MW01404578

on *their* own *terms*

on *their* own *terms*

how one woman's choice to die
helped me understand my father's suicide

Levellers Press

AMHERST, MASSACHUSETTS

Copyright © 2019 Laurie Loisel

All rights reserved including the right of reproduction in whole or in part in any form.

All photos of Lee Hawkins credit Carol Lollis, courtesy of the *Daily Hampshire Gazette*. All photos of Paul Loisel courtesy of the author.

Published by Levellers Press, Amherst, Massachusetts
Printed in the United States of America
ISBN 978-1-945473-98-2

For Lee and Paul, with love and appreciation

INTRODUCTION	9
A man and his children	15
Paul makes a plan	27
"He fucking did it."	37
Three extraordinary things	49
A surprising letter	57
A vibrant life	67
Lee makes a plan	79
Accepting Lee's choice	91
Lee's goodbye	99
After Lee	113
Scattering Paul's ashes	123
ADDENDA	133
DISCUSSION PROMPTS	155
ACKNOWLEDGMENTS	161

Introduction

MY FATHER, PAUL LOISEL, AND MY FRIEND LEE HAWKINS didn't have a lot in common. She was a well-educated, well-read public school teacher, a native Californian who spent her adult life on the East Coast, a Unitarian Universalist with a passion for social justice. He was a lifelong resident of working-class central Maine, a jack-of-all-trades who painted houses, delivered milk and raised chickens for a living, and grew to detest the church of his childhood with a passion that was almost evangelical. They shared these traits: Both preferred to fix problems rather than complain about them. Both were feisty, stubborn and independent. In their own ways, both loved nothing more than to challenge conventional thinking. And at the end of their lives, they refused to let aging take them on what they viewed as an inevitable journey of decline and dependence. Both made decisions, and then took actions, that ended their lives.

✷

I met Lee Hawkins in the late 1990s at the Unitarian Society of Northampton and Florence, where we both were members. A diminutive, white-haired woman with an infectious smile and a hearty laugh, she possessed a self-confidence, both intellectually and socially, that, to me, bordered on intimidating. She was utterly at ease speaking her mind in private and in public.

Lee had moved from Staten Island to Northampton, a small city in western Massachusetts, drawn in part to the vitality of our Unitarian congregation. She quickly became an indelible presence, well-known for standing up at our annual meeting to comment on a procedure or action under consideration. She never held back — even if some people wanted things to move along more quickly or smoothly, or found her comments picky or inconvenient. Sometimes she'd speak up about process if she believed a vote hadn't been transparent enough. More often she'd speak up about racial equality or social justice, matters dear to her heart. She believed that our largely white congregation needed more people of color, and said so. She felt we weren't working hard enough to make that happen, that we should do more. She also strongly believed Unitarians should be working for social justice all the time, not just showing up for Sunday services.

When her body began failing, she took to using a walker, but that didn't stop her from traveling far during our community greeting on Sunday mornings. She glided smoothly through the aisles, saying hello, with her broad, toothy smile, to anyone she'd never met before.

I admired the way she cut through the space between people to shake hands and make a connection — a real connection. I observed all these qualities about Lee and accepted her warm handshake and expectant greeting when she made her way to me.

Little did I know then that we would develop a friendship kindled by her admiration for my father, who killed himself with a gunshot in a parking lot outside a police station in Hallowell, Maine, on December 3, 2012. He was eighty-three. He was not sick, nor was he depressed. He did it to avoid what he saw as the ravages of age, which in his mind included a loss of independence that he found intolerable. Though he had no dementia diagnosis, and no known family history of the disease, his greatest fear was a diminishing of his mind.

I didn't know then that Lee, for similar reasons, had her own plan to avoid certain eventualities her own aging might bring. Lee died in her own home on September 2, 2014, at age ninety, after carrying out that plan. Unlike my father's violent death, hers was peaceful, brought about because she stopped taking in food and water, a method rarely discussed, but common enough that it has an acronym: VSED, voluntarily stopping eating and drinking.

Neither Lee nor her doctor saw this as an act of suicide, but as something far more natural. While most definitely legal — it certainly is anybody's right to stop taking in food and liquid — VSED remains fairly unusual. At the hospice organization caring for Lee, it was unusual enough that it prompted officials to develop protocols for people who choose to take that route.

To be clear, VSED is not assisted suicide. Many states — including Massachusetts, where I live — have engaged in robust debates about assisted suicide legislation, sometimes referred to as Death with Dignity laws or medical aid in dying. These laws apply only to qualifying patients with terminal diagnoses who request and obtain life-ending medication from a doctor.

To date, nine states have adopted such laws. Maine, where my father lived, did so in June 2019. Massachusetts, through ballot initiatives and legislative sessions, including some as I write this in 2019, has considered Death with Dignity measures half a dozen times.

In the months before my father killed himself, Massachusetts was in the midst of a deeply divisive Death with Dignity ballot initiative that wound up defeated by a fifty-one to forty-nine percent vote margin. Even though he was living in Maine, he followed the debate with avid interest and was dismayed when it was defeated. On that same ballot, voters approved a measure to legalize medical marijuana. My father taped to the wall of his small apartment a political cartoon showing a doctor addressing a terminally ill patient, "I can't really help you much, but I can offer you some legal weed."

But the fact is, Maine's now-adopted Death with Dignity law would not have helped my father. Nor, had there been one in Massachusetts, would it have been any help to Lee. People like Lee and my father — elderly people facing the slow and natural decline of old age with no terminal diagnosis — generally find no recourse in assisted suicide laws. They fall into a category that no legislation has addressed and many families find excruciating to discuss. So the question remains: Do people have a right to hasten their deaths when living has become something they no longer want?

In September 2015, I wrote a three-day series about Lee Hawkins that addressed this question. It was published in the *Daily Hampshire Gazette*, where I then worked as the Northampton-based paper's managing editor for news. The stories chronicled her decision to bring about her death and included the perspectives of Lee and her family, the healthcare workers caring for her, and the friends who accompanied her on a journey of her choosing.

When I met Lee, of course, I couldn't have imagined any of that. I had no clue that I would be among those surrounding her as she prepared to — and then actively did — bring about her death. And I had no idea that my friendship with Lee and her children through that process would help me come to terms with my father's death.

A man and his children

IF ANY SINGLE THING defined and organized my father's life, it was his children. He was always a hard worker, though he had no career to speak of. His work life was a mishmash of jobs selected in part because he could be his own boss. In retrospect, I see that most of the decisions he made were based around his children. Even, in his mind anyway, his decision to end his life by suicide.

My father was the middle of three boys raised in Waterville, Maine, a mill town in the central part of the state. Like many people in that small city, his grandparents emigrated from Quebec. His parents spoke Canadian French at home. They were devout Catholics. We grandchildren referred to them by the French words for grandparents: Mémère and Pépère (pronounced Mem-MAY and Pep-PAY.)

Pépère worked his way up to be foreman at a Scott Paper Company plant. Mémère kept a house neat as a pin and was a strict, if loving, disciplinarian to my father and his two brothers, Don and Carl. She kept her eye on my grandfather, too. A sweet and affable man, he was prone to drinking too much when not at work. My grandmother regularly watered down the bottle of gin he kept in the cabinet under the sink. Pépère knew this, so he doubled up on what he drank to account for it.

None of this was ever discussed, of course. Nor was the time Pépère, who was, I'm certain, intoxicated, fell and hurt his head while walking to the boardwalk on a trip with my sisters and me to Hampton Beach. Mémère cleaned the cut, gave Pépère the stink eye for a few hours, and never spoke of it again.

When the grownups wanted to speak privately, they didn't leave the room or whisper — they spoke French. There was no effort or desire to teach me, my siblings or our cousins to speak their language. My father would later tell a grandchild interviewing him for a school report that he was ashamed of his heritage. He felt speaking French was something to hide, not to pass down to the next generation.

In 1946, when he was eighteen, my father joined the U. S. Navy for a two-year tour. It was the year after World War II ended and he saw no action, but he did visit parts of the world he otherwise never would have seen, including Egypt. A picture of him there, sitting atop a camel, hung in our grandparents' house for many years. That tour in the Navy entitled him to the GI Bill, which paid for him to earn a business degree at Thomas Junior College in Waterville, the highest level of education he would obtain.

In 1952, he married my mother, a fun-loving beauty, also French Canadian, who had been raised by a single mother on welfare. They settled twenty miles south of Waterville in the state capital, Augusta. Their marriage produced five children; I was the fifth and youngest.

Paul, right, with a U. S. Navy buddy, ca. 1946.

My father worked as a milk delivery man and then a traveling salesman. He was a charismatic and friendly man who thrived on contact with people, which meant door-to-door sales were solidly in his wheelhouse.

For many years, he sold Baby Butlers, a peculiar piece of baby furniture akin to a high chair, but with a larger table area that was — as my father would pledge to prospective customers — much, much safer than a traditional high chair.

He wasn't above the sort of thing that gives salesmen a bad name. He would go to the state fairs that pop up all over Maine as summer nears its end. There, he would demonstrate the advantages of Baby Butlers and raffle one off free to a person whose name was drawn from those who put their names and addresses on a piece of paper and dropped them into a box. When it was time to pull the name, one of his children would do the honors. At each fair, the name pulled was "Ethel Violet." She just happened to be our Aunt Ethel. My father would then use the names and addresses to go out selling. He did make cold calls, but this was much more effective.

Marlene and Paul in Augusta, Maine, ca. 1951.

Our family followed the path set by my grandparents, which was to center our lives around the Catholic Church and home life. My brothers were altar boys. We attended Mass every Sunday and at midnight on Christmas Eve, after which we'd return home to dine on tourtière, a French meat pie.

We went to confession, where I would make up infractions to tell the priest. Afterwards, we recited whatever prayers the priest had instructed us to say as penance. We participated in Stations of the Cross during the Easter season. We attended St. Mary's Catholic School, directly across from our house on Lincoln Street, where I'd wave to my grandmother on the porch when lining up to enter the building.

Shortly after my birth, my mother, always impulsive and childlike (according to those who knew her as a younger woman), developed a severe mental illness that became highly disruptive to family life. She experienced episodes of mania and spent periods of time in the Maine State Hospital, where we visited her. At home, she became increasingly entwined with the church, developed an outsized religiosity and tended to bring the priests into disagreements with my father. Under her watch, we said the rosaries at night in the living room, kneeling in front of couches and chairs with our elbows resting on the seats. There was a lot of foot-fighting among the children during those endless and boring prayer sessions.

When my parents divorced in the early '60s, she retained custody of the five of us, even though it was clear we were too much for her tenuous mental state. But those were not times when fathers contested custody of their children.

My mother's mother, Grammy Cote, moved in with us, which brought some stability, though my three brothers (whom we called "the boys" as if they were one entity) were too much for her. She was morbidly obese and had a heart of gold. I loved nothing more than to perch on the edge of her knee, turning her ample belly into my beanbag chair.

But our father was never far away. He regularly stopped by with bags of groceries, staying on to make dinner. He lived with his parents, probably because he was spending most of his money on us. He bought a camp on East Pond in Oakland,

From left to right: Paul; Laurie's godparents, Joe Hanley and Suzanne Bourque; Marlene Loisel; with Laurie on baptism day in 1960.

Loisel family picture, from left: Dan, Michaela, Marlene holding Laurie, Tim, Paul and Alan, ca. 1963.

where we spent many summer weekends. When he remarried six years later, the boys, by then teenagers, eagerly moved in with our father and new stepmother, Rose. At our urging, my father filed for custody of my sister Michaela and me. This led to a family services investigation and a series of court hearings. After several months, a judge awarded custody to my father based on my mother's inability to adequately care for us.

By this time, my father had sold the camp, bought a large, rambling house and decided to try his hand at chicken farming. For a time, our family life felt pretty normal. Rose had been a single mother with a young daughter, Mondy, whom he adopted. He and Rose soon had another child, Melissa, bringing us to a family of seven children. We fell away from the church, completing the unraveling that began when priests tried to instruct our father about how to deal with a mentally ill wife. For my father this would become a lifelong animosity. While the rest of us didn't share the depth of his hatred for the church, none of his children ever stepped foot in a Catholic Church again except to attend funerals.

My father purchased a chicken farm on sixty-three acres in Pittston, a small town not far from Augusta. He and Rose became contract chicken farmers, which meant they raised broiling hens for sale in grocery stores for a company that slaughtered and marketed them. My father and Rose tended 72,000 chickens, delivered to the farm at a few hours old and taken away nine weeks later, when they were large enough for slaughter. A crew arrived in the dark of night to retrieve the fully grown chickens. My father hired a crew of neighborhood teenagers to clear the barn of nine weeks' worth of manure and urine-soaked sawdust, a process we called "cleanout." Five days later, crews delivered another batch of hours-old chicks to start the cycle again.

We also tended cows, pigs, horses and large vegetable gardens. We opened Loisel's Vegetable Stand, a busy roadside enterprise where my sister Mondy and I earned 20 percent commission on all sales. My father developed chummy relationships with nearby farmers, a couple of them Russian immigrants who spoke no English, from whom he purchased vegetables when the pace of sales outgrew our gardens. I loved joining him for visits to their sprawling gardens, watching him walk through the rows, savoring a ripe tomato as if it were an apple while he admired their hard work. They seemed to easily communicate with each other, despite the language difference.

As a dad, he could be fun, making even boring Saturday chores seem like a game. Bringing the trash to the dump, he'd sing, to the tune of "The Lone Ranger" theme song: "To the dump, to the dump, to the dump, dump, dump!" When he made soup, as he often did on Sunday afternoons, it was a big production. Pulling out the largest pot in the cupboard, he'd stand over it, yelling "boil, boil, boil!" to the delight of my visiting friends.

But this blended family was no Brady Bunch. My mother's mental illness progressed, at times manifesting in delusions and intense paranoia. During her periods of lucidity, I spent weekends with her but even without delusions she was never parental or nurturing. I dreaded those weekends, which for me, was a source of anguish and guilt, though I never talked about it until years later. Therapy?

Not a chance. In the Loisel family culture, that was something for whiners and slackers.

One of my brothers developed a serious mental illness, which my father believed was behavior caused by the pot he smoked. In their teen years, two of my three brothers gave my father a run for his money. His parenting style for that age group, a mix of authoritarianism and shame, was less than effective. And my father, like his father, was a heavy drinker. While he continued to be a hard worker and provider, drinking beer — Schlitz, not the microbrew kind — was central to his life. In later years, I suspected that he chose work where he could be his own boss partly to enable that drinking habit.

※

In the early 1980s — when my older siblings were long gone and I was away at college — the chicken industry in Maine collapsed fairly rapidly, driven by market forces that pushed the business to Southern states.

Many Maine chicken farmers lost livelihoods and homes. My father — always one for ideas that veered toward outlandish — tried to reimagine his farm as a different sort of business. Could the barn become a mushroom-growing operation? (That might have been a hit now, but back then it was an odd idea.) An indoor mall? A porn theater? None of these ideas ever saw the light of day and the hulking silver barn sat idle. Stress related to the failure of the farm, abetted by his drinking, led my father and Rose to divorce. A while later, when the holder of the farm's mortgage tried to take the property and relocate my father to a small ranch house, he flatly refused. "This is my fucking farm and I'm not going," he told them angrily. In the end, they negotiated a deal. The bank took sixty acres of his land, forced him to tear down the barn to sell the lumber for scrap, leaving him with the house, three acres, and a mortgage he could afford.

After that loss, he tried different schemes to make money — he once sank several thousand dollars into a large tent filled with liquidation inventory that he sold by the side of the highway. It was a flop. And there was the notorious period when, living alone in the house, he essentially operated a brothel from our family home. He called it a massage parlor. This was short-lived, and rarely talked about. Even for my father, I found this one almost too preposterous to be true. I was not around and I could never bring myself to ask him about it, though according to family members, it really happened. My stepmother and youngest sister, who had moved into an apartment in town, were mortified. One of my brothers called my father to ream him out, and the massage parlor was no more.

Eventually, Dad settled into a job as a delivery clerk and office manager at a grocery distribution company, which enabled him to snag ample supplies of personal hygiene products to give to his children. He would not attempt another business until he started, of all things, the Maine Cremation Society.

Paul makes a plan

IN HIS SEVENTIES, my father became intensely focused on cremation. As longtime Catholics, our extended family was big on funeral homes with open-casket visiting hours, Catholic Masses and priest-led burials. Our dad wasn't remotely interested in any of that. Cremation — simple, direct, uncomplicated — was for him. And the more he learned, the more enthusiastic he was.

I trace this in part to his strong desire never to be a burden to others. He paid in advance for cremation packages for himself as well as for his two ex-wives, my mother and stepmother. Neither had assets, and he did not want their burial costs to fall to his kids.

Once he'd lined up those packages, he began looking more deeply into the funeral business and cremation options. He believed people were overcharged when they buried their loved ones, especially at a time when grief was raw, clouding any critical analysis of a deal. He also came to believe the whole funeral business was one big racket. Nevertheless, he wanted in on that racket.

That's why, in the twilight of his life, he developed one more questionable get-rich scheme: the Maine Cremation Society. With a vanity license plate on his car that read "CREMATE," he traveled to senior centers and other places older people congregate to educate them about the benefits of cremation and the importance of planning ahead.

Once again, he was a door-to-door salesman, traveling around the state, giving presentations in the community rooms of retirement homes. For a one-hundred-dollar membership fee, people could join the Maine Cremation Society, which entitled them to his expertise in handling all the paperwork needed to sign people up for cremation arrangements well ahead of death. He thought this was a brilliant marketing strategy and loved to tell us stories about his presentations and his successes in convincing people of the value of cremation. He felt this was a public service, and if he made a little money off the deal, all the better.

He approached a couple of funeral homes to see if they wanted to contract him to sell their services. None of them did. At least one thought what he was doing might be fraudulent and reported him to the Maine attorney general. Our father thought what he was doing was perfectly legal — or at least no more fraudulent than the funeral home business itself.

Vowing to fight the charge, he sought out all the free legal advice he could find. That included visiting the office of my brother-in-law, an assistant attorney general handling murder appeals in Maine. He did this without an appointment. It didn't matter that this was in no way his son-in-law's area of expertise.

When the threatened letter from the AG's office came, he brought it to family gatherings to read aloud, pick apart and consider options. Sit back and enjoy retirement, we told him, even though sitting still was not in his nature. It was a relief to my siblings and me when he shut down the Maine Cremation Society, though for him, I think it represented a painful loss of purpose.

Despite my father's focus on that particular end-of-life consideration, he was otherwise very much engaged in life. He took up ballroom dancing in his sixties, spending several nights a week out on the dance circuit. He made new friends and met a cadre of dance partners. He hung a wooden sign on his door that read "Gone Dancing," and he was gone a lot: to dance events and classes around Maine, Massachusetts and New York. He took a two-day Argentine tango workshop in Northampton. Over time, he became a skilled, sought-after dance partner. He once applied to work on a cruise ship as a ballroom dancing partner. We all believed his quirky personality and unusual appearance — completely bald, no eyelashes or eyebrows, and short like me at just five feet, two inches — may have been why he'd gotten not so much as a callback after his initial interview.

He enrolled in courses at a community college, including one on world religions, in which he was thrilled to discover that he was an atheist. This was a momentous realization. He spoke about his atheism with almost boyish excitement, as if he couldn't believe that he could simply decide he did not believe in God and that a church, once the cornerstone of his life, was yet another corrupt institution.

He was keenly interested in politics, tending to vote Democratic, though like many ornery Mainers, he harbored libertarian leanings. Never much of a reader as a younger man, he became a regular at the Maine State Library. He preferred nonfiction, particularly history books and exposés of the Catholic Church. He also tried a few novels. A librarian who liked to chat with him during his visits there wrote to me after his death to say that a popular book he'd put on order had arrived. It was none other than *Fifty Shades of Grey*.

During this period, he also began thinking ahead to the turns his life might take as he aged, prompting him to make plans and even lifestyle changes. Though he was an active senior with no known health issues, he put his name on a list for subsidized senior housing. When an apartment opened up sooner than expected, he accepted the offer. His girlfriend at the time had no interest, so he left the small trailer they shared and moved into a senior apartment complex on a bus line, in case the day came when he could not drive.

He made friends at the complex, where he was the picture of youthful vitality. When he went outside to pick up his newspaper in the early mornings, he gathered up all his neighbors' papers, delivering them around the building to their apartment doors. In winter, he cleared snow off the cars of tenants who found the chore too difficult. True to form, he was once again the life of the party.

Only later did we come to understand that other aspects of life in senior housing scared him. He saw people aging up close, witnessing the decline of many people who'd become

Loisel sisters Michaela, Melissa, Laurie and Mondy in a playful moment with Paul.

his friends. He cringed as he watched frailty rob them of their independence and cognitive abilities. He feared this was in his future.

Meanwhile, his body was becoming weaker, though he downplayed it. He developed a circulation problem in his legs that forced him to cut way back on his dancing and then stop entirely. This was a loss he endured, but never discussed. A heart arrhythmia required a pacemaker. He developed colon polyps that led his doctors at the VA hospital in Augusta to send him to Boston for surgery. For a man who took pride in not going to doctors, these ailments were signs of mortality.

In the summer of 2012, when he was eighty-three, as we were sitting by the lake at my brother's camp in Belgrade, Maine, my father told me he was thinking about killing himself. I was surprised and concerned, and said so. He assured me this was not imminent.

He explained that he viewed this as a rational choice if he felt his life was no longer worth living. He had come up with a method he believed was sound and sensible and it was this: He would drive to a police station, park in the lot, and shoot himself. I have to admit, I thought it was the stupidest idea I'd ever heard. But he had thought it through. He felt it addressed some of the big problems with suicide. Nobody, he pointed out, would find him dead in his apartment. Police officers are trained to handle these situations, he told me.

Clearly, he was approaching this in a rational way. Still, I couldn't tell if this was just another crazy idea that wouldn't see the light of day or if he was really serious. He had been a hunter as a younger man, and always owned a shotgun. As someone who'd lived on a farm for years, he thought it was completely acceptable to put animals out of their misery this way, so why not himself?

I am not opposed to assisted suicide — and I believe people have a right to make choices about their end-of-life care, even the manner of their death. However, I abhor guns

Paul with his grandchildren, from left: Laurie's niece Abby Loisel, and Laurie's children, Sydney and Simon, ca. 1995.

and he knew that. I never called his idea stupid, but I did challenge his thinking. There are other, more humane methods, if and when that time comes, I told him. I'll do some research to get more information, I said.

"Using a gun is a violent way to die, Dad," I said. "Whoever finds you will be traumatized."

When I asked why this was on his mind when so many interests and activities kept him busy, he confessed to feeling the pain and limitations of aging. I knew that while running an errand in his car, he'd hit the gas instead of the brakes and plowed into a shop window. Thankfully, nobody was hurt, but the experience shook him up. He could no longer walk the entire length of Walmart because of pain in his legs, he said.

Still, he was making adjustments. He purchased a three-wheel bike with a large basket on the back and a smooth, easy glide, so he could get to the nearby shopping center if driving became impossible.

I could see his ambivalence and focused on that, reminding him that he still had a lot to live for.

I told him that his grandchildren and his children would be anguished and traumatized if he shot himself. I suggested he take his time to consider many other options. I repeated my offer to research those options.

He listened respectfully. At the time, I thought he saw all my points and realized that his idea was a bad one.

"He fucking did it."

SEVERAL MONTHS LATER, in November of 2012, I planned a visit to my family in Maine. I'd stay at my sister's Hallowell home, but my main purpose would be to spend time with my father, a few miles away in Augusta. As that early December trip drew near, my older brother, Dan, who lives in Texas, called me.

"I think Dad might be making an actual plan to kill himself," he said. A former longtime ER doc, my brother is not easily riled or prone to hyperbole.

I told him about my conversation in August. Dan said they had a similar one over the summer. His plan had not seemed imminent. "What's changed?" I asked.

Dan explained that our father had called to ask if he wanted a particular piece of furniture he owned and he was making decisions about who in the family should receive certain items after he died.

"Okay, well, I'm going to visit him next week. I'll talk to him about this," I said.

"I'll join you," Dan replied.

That's when I knew it was really serious. I still couldn't believe Dad would follow through. But this new information was troubling enough that I initiated a family dinner for my brother, father and sisters — Michaela, Mondy and Melissa — all of whom lived nearby. Our oldest brother Tim lived in Vermont so he wouldn't be there. But for those who could, it was time to take stock together.

The morning I was to drive up to Maine, a friend on the treadmill next to me at the gym asked about my weekend plans and I spilled: "I'm going to visit my family, but it's turning out that we're going to have a kind of intervention with our father because he's talking about killing himself." I'd hoped saying the words out loud would make it real. Instead, I wound up feeling that I had exaggerated and overshared with an unsuspecting, if sympathetic, friend just trying to get in a morning workout.

I timed my departure from Northampton to pass through Portland to pick up Danny at the airport. As we pulled onto the highway, I said: "Tell me the exact words Dad said that made you concerned. Every word."

The red flag had been the inventory our father had made of his few possessions, but mainly, he said, it was a feeling: Dad was signaling that he was prepared to act. It wasn't a vague, far-off idea. He believed it had evolved into a solid plan.

We both felt he was still too young and healthy to consider such a drastic act. But was he downplaying the amount of pain he experienced? I'd noticed he'd been forgetful over the summer. Did that mean he was suffering the cognitive decline he feared? When it came to health concerns, he was more apt to minimize his problems than exaggerate them.

Dan and I agreed the method he'd described to us over the summer was crazy. But since he'd been known to come up with some crazy ideas, we had to take this seriously.

That evening, my brother, my sister Michaela and I had dinner with our father at his apartment. He'd made Dan's favorite meal, spaghetti and meatballs and salad. He even had tourtière in the oven. I scanned his apartment for clues. A sticky note on the wall reminded him of a medical appointment after Christmas. That's a good sign, I thought. He ate well, seemed happy to see us, and appeared to be fully engaged.

I brought up his talk of suicide from the summer. I reminded him that though I had been planning this visit for a while, Dan had joined us because he was concerned.

"What's going on, Dad?" I asked.

He looked a little sheepish. His response was a mix of bluster, humor and defensiveness, mostly focused on an it's-my-life angle. We assured him that we were well aware it was his life and that we respected it was his choice alone. We simply wanted to talk through options so that he wouldn't make a decision about life and death based on conditions that might be changeable or easily fixable. We also wanted to make sure he wasn't depressed — another potentially fixable problem. He agreed to see a therapist at the VA. He even said I could join him. I promised to make an appointment as soon as possible, which I did two days later.

Slowly, with gentle prodding, he disclosed over dinner that night other experiences weighing heavily on him. A neighbor on his floor had suffered a debilitating stroke and was in a wheelchair, unable to talk or communicate in other ways. Stories like these clearly preoccupied him.

I wondered if taking care of business might help him feel more settled, the way his making arrangements for cremation seemed to years earlier. I also thought talking about his life might be therapeutic. So I asked him if he wanted me to write his obituary, since I'd written so many at the paper. This way an obit he had approved would be ready when needed — far down the road, I stressed.

He thought this was a great idea. This was how it came to be that Michaela, Dan, my father and I sat together at his kitchen table while I wrote his obituary. This may sound morbid; it was anything but. I asked questions and typed away on his new iPad. By turns hilarious, poignant and educational, our back-and-forth, with Michaela and Dan joining in, prompted deeper conversations about his life.

The rest of the weekend was filled with activity, including brunch at Slates, our favorite restaurant, and other shared meals. Our time together was punctuated by a lot of sitting around and talking, going to the movies, reading or watching sports on TV, and making plans for the next meal.

When my father became an enthusiastic reader, he started writing down in a notebook the titles of all the books he read. He showed us the list with some pride. As we talked, I watched him to evaluate if he seemed suicidal, which, in my estimation, he did not. He was animated, fully present and eager to talk about big ideas near to his heart.

On a gray afternoon, we took him to see the movie *Lincoln*, during which I stole glances at him as he sat next to me in the theater. He seemed absorbed in the story, didn't even nod off once. It was snowing when we left the theater and ran into my youngest sister, Melissa, who'd been at a different movie. We laughed and hugged, with large, wet flakes falling on us, and said we'd see one another the next evening at the family dinner I was cooking.

The next morning my father came over to my sister's house while she was at work, and I prepared dinner. Dan was reading in the living room. My father hung around the kitchen while I assembled a traditional Thanksgiving dinner. It was not long after Thanksgiving and we were getting together as a family.

"That's such a nice meal you're making," he said, while I prepared the turkey for the oven, cut up butternut squash and potatoes, and started on the pumpkin pie. "You're going all out."

That evening over dinner, with six of us at the table, we did a little catching up before I broached the subject at hand.

"So, some of you know Dad has been talking about suicide," I said. This was shocking news for Melissa, though everyone else acknowledged that he'd brought the subject up with them, too.

"We're wondering, Dad, if there are things we can do that will make your life easier," I said. The others joined in, asking if there were problems we could help him address. Was he tired of the harsh Maine winters? Would he want to spend a few months in Texas with Danny?

When somebody suggested hiring a housecleaner for him, he retorted: "I want to make my own fucking bed."

We were gentle. We all told him we loved him and very

much wanted him around. I reminded him that after sitting with my mother for her peaceful death eighteen months prior, I'd realized that if possible, I'd want to be with him when he died. He was quiet and attentive. It seemed to me he was considering everything we were saying.

We offered solutions. If he was feeling lonely, we would happily spend more time with him. Each of us told him this. I said I'd take time off work to go on a road trip with him. "It would be fun, Dad," I promised. Fun always appealed to him.

Dinner wrapped up around 9:30. When we hugged goodbye, I reminded him I would be picking him up the next day to bring Dan to the Portland airport.

"We can go out for lunch afterwards," I said.

He smiled. I thought he was agreeing.

My sister Michaela happened to be upstairs when he left. He looked up the stairway, kissed two fingers and waved up to her. She waved back and said goodbye.

We all came away thinking we'd influenced him. That morning I'd made the therapy appointment at the VA, where I presumed we might discuss some of the ideas we had brainstormed at the dinner table. After he'd left, I called my partner, Lydia, back home in Northampton to report the news.

"I think it was a successful intervention," I said. "I think it's going to be okay."

I should have realized there was one clue things were not as they seemed: My father had not had a drop of alcohol during dinner that night.

Hours later, I awoke to see my brother and sister standing at the foot of my bed. My sister was silent. My brother spoke in the characteristic calm and even tone perfected in the ER. "Laurie. The Hallowell police were just here. Dad committed suicide."

I'm no screamer. It's a bizarre feeling to hear screaming and then realize it came from your own mouth. Perhaps I should not have been shocked, but I was. My whole system went into overdrive, with a whirring in my head that made it difficult to think or feel anything. Immediately feeling sick, experiencing waves of nausea and sudden diarrhea, I sat on the floor of the bathroom to call our younger sisters, Mondy and Melissa, both initially speechless. We hung up the phone. One after the other, they phoned back to say they were coming over.

I called Lydia. "He fucking did it," I said. "I can't believe it." Our son, Simon, was home. Lydia relayed the news to him while I was on the phone.

The next hours unfolded. Someone put on coffee. We dissected every detail of our dinner table conversation. At 4:45 A.M., Melissa and I drove three miles to the police station in the center of town. We needed to hear for ourselves precisely what the police knew. The officer on duty was kind as he ushered us in and offered us two seats in front of his gray metal desk where paperwork was spread out in front of him. Melissa and I sat holding hands as he told us what transpired that night. At 11:38 P.M., a police dispatcher received an emergency call from a man who had found a body on the ground next to a car in the Hallowell police station parking lot, obviously dead, with a gun beside him. When police ran the registration of the car, they discovered that at 11 P.M., Paul Loisel, the owner, had driven to the police station in Augusta, where his vehicle hit a curb. An officer approached him to see if he was okay. After that, they surmised, he drove 1.6 miles to the Hallowell department, where he achieved his grim goal.

A few hours later, we all went together to break the news first to Rose and then to his former longtime girlfriend, Rita.

We were perplexed he hadn't left so much as a goodbye note. Later, when Danny and I went to the bank to see what he'd stored in a safe deposit box, we found a receipt for a shotgun he'd bought in November. Stapled to it was a handwritten note declaring that he had made this purchase on his own, with no help from anyone. The intent was clear. He did not want anyone thinking that his children had any knowledge of or involvement in his suicide.

"That's the note he left?" I said to Dan as we left the bank. It felt so horribly impersonal and I couldn't help but feel bitter, thinking he was completely ignoring the impact of his act on us. The lack of communication was as hurtful as what he'd done.

Later that day, Dan retrieved our father's green Subaru from the lot where police had towed it. Employees there were sympathetic and didn't charge us for the tow. He took it to a car wash and then parked it in the back of my sister Michaela's driveway, where it sat unused for the next six days.

That night, two men, strangers to us, stopped by with a large bunch of flowers. They were apologetic for interrupting our evening. They explained that they had discovered our father's body in downtown Hallowell. They cried and offered condolences. We cried and apologized profusely that they had been put through something so traumatic. Boy was Dad wrong about this, I thought. How could he possibly have thought his suicide wouldn't traumatize those around him, even strangers?

The next day, I pulled out the partially written obituary to finish it. The *Kennebec Journal* had published a brief news story that an Augusta man had been found dead of a self-inflicted gunshot outside the Hallowell police station. We saw no reason to conceal that information in the obituary. I knew this was unusual and likely to raise questions in the newsroom, so I phoned the paper to let them know that the obituary I was about to send in would state that our father died by suicide. That's how we want it, I said. We didn't want any of the codes newspapers traditionally use: "died suddenly," or "unexpectedly," "found dead."

We were exhausted, unable to sleep much and didn't want to be apart. Friends stopped by with food. My friends from the paper ordered up a meal from a nearby restaurant and had it delivered to us one night. Back home, Lydia went to our daughter Sydney's college dorm room to deliver the news in person, and told our friends in Northampton what had occurred.

We cleared out his apartment, easily making decisions about who would get what. My father didn't have much and what he did have was of little value, so this was easy. I kept his TV, a nightstand, a dark green L. L. Bean flannel shirt and several pairs of his shoes — we wore the same size. While we sorted and cleaned, his neighbors stopped by to offer condolences and tell us how much they enjoyed him. As instructed in a note he left us in his apartment, we gave one of his neighbors his hearing aids. He was practical and frugal to the end.

Meanwhile, using my sister's house as our headquarters, we made arrangements. We planned a memorial service, found someone to cater lunch afterwards, and enlisted a friend to make a program for the service.

One thing we didn't need to do was figure out burial details. He was cremated, just as he had arranged so many years before.

Three extraordinary things

THE WEEKEND OF OUR FATHER'S MEMORIAL SERVICE, three things transpired, each of which we never could have imagined. Each of them was simply hard to believe.

We held the service at the Unitarian Universalist Church in Augusta, where my sister was a member. We knew our father wouldn't want anything particularly churchy or reverent — and neither did any of us. We planned the memorial carefully, with music, songs, poetry, readings and words from his children, grandchildren and family friends. My sister's ex-husband officiated. We talked about our father's life, telling stories that pulled no punches, drawing much laughter from our friends. We also did not shy away from the specific manner of his death or how sad it made us all.

We invited people in the room to speak if they felt so inclined. Some people we had never met stood to tell stories about our father. Most were anecdotes that illustrated his zest for life. It was this characteristic of his colorful personality that caused people to be shocked by his suicide. A librarian described how much she enjoyed his visits to the Maine State

Library, where they would chat about the books he read or might want to read. Many people said he was the most full-of-life person they knew.

Without euphemisms, we talked about his suicide and the stigma of suicide. As his children, even while we wished it hadn't been his choice at this time, we said we didn't think it should hold a stigma, not for him and not for his family.

As the service drew to a close, my sister Michaela stood up to address everyone. In unplanned remarks, she said: "I will not feel shame about my father's suicide."

With that, my brother Tim jumped up to hug her. Then Melissa was on her feet. One after the other, Mondy, Dan and I joined them in a spontaneous group hug. When we turned around, everyone in the room was on their feet, clapping. It was an extraordinary moment.

Afterwards, as people headed out toward the social room for lunch, our aunt asked for a private moment with us. Joanne, who had driven up from New Hampshire with her daughter, had been married to Uncle Don, our father's older brother, who had died two years prior at age eighty-two.

Uncle Don had been buried with a big Catholic mass and funeral in Lawrence, Massachusetts, to which Michaela and I accompanied our father. After their younger brother's premature death by heart attack fifteen years prior, Carl, Dad and Uncle Don had been close. We knew the loss of his older brother would be hard on him, so we wanted to be with him for the funeral.

As we clustered awkwardly together in the pews after our father's memorial service, Joanne disclosed something entirely unexpected: Uncle Don had not died of natural causes, as everyone had been led to believe. She explained that Uncle Don had a routine medical appointment the day he died, for which she had arranged a car service to ferry him to the office (he had long before stopped driving). It was a work day for Joanne, and she planned to meet him at the appointment. She phoned Uncle Don that morning to remind him the driver would be there soon and she would see him at the office, to which he replied, "Yes, it will be over soon." Only in retrospect did she understand the meaning of his odd phrasing.

When Don did not arrive at the doctor's office at the appointed time, Joanne called the car service only to be told they were running late. And then, as she watched for the car, snow falling outside, she saw a police cruiser arrive. Soon, a police officer tapped on her shoulder, asking to speak to her in private. She thought he might be there to report a car accident involving Don. The officer informed her that Uncle Don had been found dead. He had killed himself, using a gun, in their backyard.

In shock, Joanne, also a lifelong practicing Catholic, made a hasty decision she would come to regret. Nobody should know how her husband had died. She wanted everyone to remember Uncle Don as the upbeat, always smiling, glass-half-full man he'd always seemed to be. "I didn't want people to think less of Don," she later told me. She kept the information secret, telling their daughter, but nobody else — not Uncle Don's two children from his first marriage, not his brother, not her own ninety-two-year-old mother.

We sat in the pews in stunned silence. Two brothers, at just about the same age, each died by suicide by gun, unbeknownst to each other. Each death carefully planned so family members would not discover them. It was extraordinary.

Joanne was certain our father had no idea about his brother's suicide. I reflected back on Uncle Don's funeral and the many conversations I had with my father about his brother. I knew without a doubt he had no inkling his older brother had killed himself. If he had, I believe he would have used that information to convince us his plan was not as crazy as we all seemed to think it was.

Joanne told us she deeply regretted her secrecy around Uncle Don's death. "One lie led to another," she said, and that made it hard to receive comfort from friends and relatives. Seeing the open way we'd dealt with our father's suicide, she said, made her realize a different path might

Loisel brothers, Carl, Paul and Don, ca. 1994

have allowed for a much healthier healing process.

At my sister's house twenty-four hours later, a third extraordinary event unfolded. We were tying up loose ends, preparing to go our separate ways after ten intense days together. My brother and sister-in-law, Kathy, had taken our father's car to run an errand. I was alone in the house when they returned.

Kathy held in her hands a thick manila envelope. She seemed a little nervous. "Laurie, we found something stuck underneath the passenger seat," she said.

I looked at the envelope, which bore my father's familiar scrawl.

"He left a note?" I shouted in disbelief. I was unaware my legs had buckled until I felt my brother holding me up from behind. Inside the envelope were several items: multiple copies of his license; his DNR; an apology to police and instructions for them that included a telephone number and address for Michaela; a note addressed "To the children I love so dearly."

Dad's letter answered some of our questions. For me, it provided comfort. The three of us sat together on the couch, my head on Kathy's shoulder while she slowly read it out loud.

"You will heal from this, I know, because the human mind mends fast and well," he'd written. He'd meant for us to have the note the night he shot himself. He'd planned it so carefully, but the note must have fallen from the passenger seat, possibly when he'd made the intercepted stop at the Augusta station where he'd faced questioning by the police. Later, the Hallowell police apparently did not search the car. Possibly they assumed he would have left a suicide note at his home, which is what we all thought, too.

"With all my love I leave you. Please find happiness together," Kathy read. "You will heal and my love will help you to heal."

The note was so loving, self-reflective and poetic that my oldest brother, Tim, questioned whether our father could possibly have been the author. I knew he was. He was always a big thinker, though he hid it from many.

"The human mind mends fast," he'd written.

I might have written "human heart" — and I believe that's what he meant. But if he had sat at his kitchen table and actually written the words "human heart," he might not have been able to carry through with his plan, even though, as he also wrote, it was a "must for me to avoid future pain."

If he'd written the words "human heart," that's right where he would have felt it. Then I think he might have realized he was breaking his own human heart as well as all of ours.

A surprising letter

THE LETTER ARRIVED IN THE MAIL on a warm day in late May 2013, more than five months after my father's suicide. I was still in the thick fog of grief. I took it from the mailbox when I went home to walk our dog, Ella, on a break from my job at the newspaper.

Opening a plain white envelope addressed in tiny script written in the shaky hand of an eighty-nine-year-old, I wondered why Lee Hawkins would be writing to me. Inside was a typed letter I would read over and over to myself, to my siblings, to my friends and even colleagues.

Lee — whom I knew from the Unitarian Society but not especially well — was responding to a column I had written for the *Daily Hampshire Gazette* two months earlier, in which I discussed my family's unusual decision to be explicit about our father's suicide in his obituary.

She told of her admiration for my father. I was floored. I'd thought and felt a lot of things about my father's suicide, none of which involved admiration. I reread the letter to see if I could understand why this gentle, vibrant woman would

Lee Hawkins at her desk in her Northampton home in 2014.

find my father's violent act admirable. She had even called him a role model.

Always my family's scribe, I'd written his obituary, starting with this paragraph: *Paul Reginald Loisel, 83, died Dec. 3 the way he lived his life — on his own terms. Paul spent a joyful evening having a belated Thanksgiving dinner with his family, during which time many stories were told and many laughs were shared. Later that night, Paul took his own life.*

The column explained why we disclosed this information in the obituary and at his memorial service: We believed his action had been his choice, that there should be no stigma attached. Tragic though it was, it was a fact.

That it had taken Lee two months after reading the column to send me a letter may be a testament to her thoughtfulness, but as likely, it was also due to the slow pace aging had ushered into her life.

"Dear Laurie, I have just reread your column about your father's death, one that is headed to my folder marked DEATH. I am going to speak to you as your father might."

She described her aversion to becoming, as she put it, "a resident of a nursing home." She explained that she'd had many conversations with her children about what she called a planned death. She also admitted her own ambivalence. Lee explained that when she'd recently broached the subject of her planned death with one of her daughters, the reaction was immediate: "'Oh, not YET.' Not surprisingly, I feel the same way! There are unfinished chores: letters to write, a will to rethink," she wrote.

She included a few sentences I would come to study: "I admire your father. He left you with so many warm feelings, as you did him. He was thoughtful in the papers he left behind .... Suicide might be a source of shame to family members if they had in some way made life unbearable for the 'victim,' clearly not the case here. To me, your father is a role model!"

I thought a lot about Lee's words and then called her. I thanked her for writing, and told her that her words had been meaningful to read.

"I'm wondering if we could get together?"

"I would like that," she said, the first of many times she would say that to me.

A few weeks later, over tea and cookies at her round, well-worn, wooden dining room table, we talked about aging, death and families. I told her I was mad at my father, angry about the violent manner of his death. She said she saw his suicide not as dysfunctional but as brave. The notion baffled me. She described her own thoughts about death after a good, long life, which she told me was a subject she'd discussed with her children over many years.

Lee, four years older than my father, was rational, clear-eyed and stable. She saw no reason to go beyond the point where she wasn't enjoying an independent life. The trick, she believed, would be knowing when that point came before it was too late to act. Your father, she told me, was afraid he'd go past that point and then be trapped in a life he didn't want.

"I understand that," she said.

Lee was a no-nonsense woman, highly practical, efficient, opinionated, politically progressive and sometimes sharp-tongued. She mentioned articles she'd read about vast sums of money spent on often fruitless medical interventions as people neared death. She believed those efforts to stave off a natural outcome — death — sometimes merely prolonged lives that involved a great deal of pain and anguish. She thought that was a travesty and often not what the dying person really wanted.

For her, there were other factors to consider. She valued her independence. She liked living on her own at a retirement village in Northampton. She felt she had an enjoyable life even without being able to drive herself around, something she decided to stop doing, she would point out to me more than once, on her own, at age eighty-six. She had friends over, and was involved with a Unitarian dinner group that met monthly for years. She attended services at her beloved Unitarian Society, and made her own meals. She was an avid follower of current events, politics, and anything involving racial justice.

In short, she cared for herself well. But Lee already knew that when she could no longer do that, she would not want to keep living. For her, a nursing home was out of the question, as was leaving Northampton to move in with her children, who lived out of state. She would rather take steps to end her life, probably by stopping eating and drinking.

I was moved by her conviction. It was so heartfelt and passionate, it seemed paradoxically life-affirming. I told her I'd like to return for another visit, to which she replied: "I would like that."

Lee Hawkins in 2015

The next visit, I asked if she would let me interview her to write a story for the *Gazette* about her end-of-life decision-making. "Well, I don't see why not," she answered. When I told her I'd like to talk to her children as well, she said that was fine with her if it was okay with them.

Over the next six weeks, I paid weekly visits to Lee, reporter's notebook in hand. My note-taking didn't inhibit her in the least. We'd chat about her childhood, her courtship with her late husband, Roger, whom she called Rog, with a soft G. We talked about all the things you're not supposed to talk about in polite company: politics, religion, death. She would tell me that she believed there was nothing after this life and that she would live on in the memories of her children, grandchildren, and friends.

One day, she told me her daughter Sue was coming to visit and invited me to join them for dinner. So it was that I met Sue Hawkins, Lee's oldest child, and Jerry Hawkins, her middle child, who was also visiting his mother. Months later, I would meet Becky, her youngest child, a teacher a few years younger than me. During dinner, Sue and Jerry told stories about their mother's ease in talking with them about the end of her life, to the point where they never needed to have The Big Talk. They simply knew her wishes.

Lee recalled how she and Rog talked frankly about their deaths. One time, she said, they filled out end-of-life questionnaires designed to help families make decisions in a calm moment, before a health crisis hits. She went to her study with her form, while Roger sat at the kitchen table to fill out his. Lee thought it was funny that she spent about five minutes while Roger spent about an hour. When Lee asked what took so long, Roger simply said he liked to think things over.

That first story I wrote about Lee detailed her thoughts and feelings about aging, medical interventions at the end of life, her ideas about planning her death and her children's reaction. It appeared on the *Gazette's* feature pages in 2013, a full year before Lee would take steps to bring about her death.

As we wrapped up our interviews, I told Lee I would miss our weekly visits and asked if we could keep them going, which delighted her.

"I would like that," she said.

I continued my habit of asking Lee a lot of questions, which she always welcomed.

"What is the hardest part about getting old?" I inquired once. She didn't have to think long. "People assume I don't want to go out and do things with them," she said.

That's when I started inviting her to do things with me. We had many Friday night dinners together. She taught me to play Anagrams, a game she loved, and we played it over and over again. At my request, she played Rummikub once, but we never played again because she didn't like it. I took her out to an *a cappella* concert, to my mother-in-law's for Thanksgiving dinner, for Chinese food with my family to celebrate her ninetieth birthday, to see my favorite movie, *The Sound of Music*, on the big screen at the Amherst Cinema on my fifty-fourth birthday.

Our friendship flourished, crossing journalistic boundaries mainly because I assumed that part of our relationship was behind us. Dropping her off after a Sunday morning service at the Unitarian Society in June of 2014, she told me something that should not have surprised me, but it did.

"I think this summer is the time to end my life — probably in August," she said.

Even though we'd discussed this endlessly, I felt at a loss for words.

I felt I owed her honesty, at least, so I finally, simply said what was true: "I respect your choice. But still, it makes me sad."

"It makes me sad too," she said, "Our friendship feels too new to be saying goodbye."

Later, I talked about my reactions with my family and friends, including some in the newsroom. Let me tell you, journalists can't help themselves: We began talking about what a rare and amazing opportunity it would be to witness and write about this type of death — not as an abstract, but as a profoundly intimate experience. My dear friend and longtime colleague, Carol Lollis, the paper's photo editor, was eager to be involved in the project.

Soon after, with some trepidation, I asked Lee what she would think about this idea. She said it didn't really matter to her, since she liked talking with me and she would be dead before any story would be published. However, she did not want to do anything to upset her children during a difficult time. If they had any objections or discomfort, we would not move forward.

I reached out to all three children, who said they were fine with me coming around and that they didn't mind all the questions I tended to ask. Sue said talking to me seemed to help clarify her thinking. They all met Carol, whose warm and direct way with people made her connections with the Hawkins family solid and allowed her to obtain the extraordinary photos that appeared in the newspaper.

We all agreed if things felt uncomfortable in any way, they could stop the project at any time.

A vibrant life*

ONE DAY IN MID-JUNE OF 2014, Lee Hawkins awakened when an aide arrived to rouse her, get her showered and dressed, and prepare her breakfast. At age ninety, Lee, a tiny woman with white, wispy hair and an infectious smile, could no longer complete these tasks on her own. But the helper left after an hour or two, and Lee was alone for the rest of the day.

Lee had a wheelchair but preferred her walker, which glided over wood floors and carpeting equally well. She made her way slowly around the house, pushing the walker, taking small steps, resting in between. It was outfitted with a basket holding important items — house phone and Rolodex, church directory, pens and pencils, combs, magnifying glass, remote control for her TV, roll of duct tape, a device to pick things up. She kept her cellphone in her pocket and an emergency call button around her neck at all times. These were the things that allowed Lee to continue living the way she wanted, alone in her own home, long after her children began wondering if she was safe.

*Reprinted from the Daily Hampshire Gazette, September 23, 2014

She had fallen so many times that she had grown fond of the EMTs who arrived when she pressed the emergency button to summon help. But she always argued the point when they wanted to take her to the emergency room.

Lee was nearing the end of her life and she was well aware of this. She had no terminal illness, other than the one we all suffer from — human mortality — but she felt her time to die was imminent. And she had a plan.

Born in 1924, Eleanor "Lee" Hawkins was raised in Carmel, California, the only child of a teacher and a grocer. After graduating from the University of California at Berkeley, she bicycled by herself around Europe in 1948 and 1949 and settled in New York City. There, Lee married Roger Hawkins, a man thirteen years her senior who had been divorced, a fact that did not please her mother.

They married in 1950, and moved to Staten Island in 1955, where they raised their three children, Sue, Jeremy and Rebecca. Roger Hawkins commuted to the city for his job as project manager for a commercial art shop.

Their large Staten Island home was a bustling hive. Lee earned her master's degree in 1962 and once her children were in school, she embarked on a career as a public school teacher. She was active in the Unitarian Church, where she found like-minded people. She organized Camp Fire Girls troops for both daughters that lasted for many years; Sue's group was so tight it had reunions in 1976 and again in 2012.

Even as she embraced life, Lee always felt comfortable talking about aging and death, subjects many treated as taboo. Even years back when she was the picture of health, she discussed her thoughts about death and the tendency of people to live long past the time when they could care for themselves. She read a lot and held strong opinions about the money spent on medical care for people at the end of life, which she felt was a waste of precious resources that could be devoted to people in poverty.

"It's a social justice issue," she'd say.

The family had a summer cottage on a lake in Sturbridge, Massachusetts. After retiring, Lee and Roger decided to leave Staten Island to move closer to their cottage and their children, who had settled in the Northeast. Her longtime best friend, Grace Ilchuck, and her family also bought a cottage on the lake, where the families summered together for many years. While searching for their new home, Lee and Roger attended a Sunday service at the Unitarian Society of Northampton and Florence on Main Street. They loved the sermon and the people they met afterwards. Somebody told them about the Lathrop Retirement Community under construction off Bridge Road. After the service, they drove to look at the complex and put a deposit down on the spot.

They moved to the new unit at the end of Golden Chain Lane in 1991. The Unitarian Society became the hub of Lee and Roger's life in Northampton. Both made connections through committee work, circle dinners, and other social activities. Roger joined a men's group where the men once decided to try being more like women by calling each other for no particular purpose, an experiment that quickly went by the boards. But the connections were strong.

When Roger died at age ninety-four in 2004 — in his obituary, his daughter Sue attributed his death to pneumonia and "a well-worn body" — members of his men's group

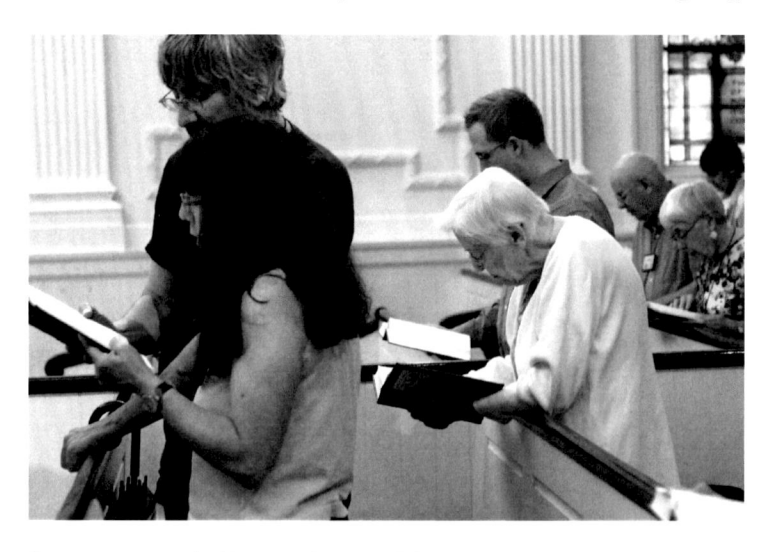

Lee at a service at the Unitarian Society of Northampton and Florence in 2014.

Lee wanted to live independently for as long as she could.

spoke at his memorial service. After his death, Lee continued her deep involvement. She was on the social justice committee and for many years was co-chair of a group that provided meals and other help for society members who became ill. When she entered into a period of increasing frailty and old age, members rallied to help her with rides to services and trips to the grocery store.

But that help wasn't enough as she aged and grew more frail. Though not one to talk about physical ailments, Lee found herself in constant pain. She was not a complainer, but there were many ways life was hard: She endured the loss of things many people consider vital to a good life. She'd stopped driving at age eighty-six. She'd lost the focus and energy to read a good book and could no longer reach down to take her shoes off before bed. She was rapidly losing the ability to hear, to get herself out of bed, or to easily open the refrigerator door to ponder lunch options.

Her children lived in New York and Vermont, each at least two hours away. Lee did not want to leave her life in Northampton, nor did she want to move in with them. She told them, as she had before, that a planned death, in her mind, was an acceptable option if she couldn't care for herself or do the things she most enjoyed, like church on Sundays. Her plan was to stop eating and drinking, a method that seemed — to her, at least — natural and peaceful.

In June of 2014, four months after Lee turned ninety, she told her daughters and some friends she'd decided the time had come to implement her plan. She felt she'd lived a good, fulfilling life, and had recently finished up some projects and gotten certain affairs in order. She did not consider this suicide. August, she said, seemed a convenient time, easier for her children to spend time with her while she died. Her children repeatedly said they supported her, but they didn't want their lives to be a factor in her decision. With a mix of cheerful bravado and sadness, her daughter Sue told her, "Your death will never be convenient."

On June 30, Lee and her daughters, Sue and Becky, met for the first time with Dr. Jeffrey Zesiger in a conference room at Northampton's Cooley Dickinson Hospital. They were in search of information. Lee wanted specific details about what it would be like to stop eating and drinking.

Zesiger, a hospice and palliative care specialist, is a soft-spoken man with short cropped gray hair and a quick smile. He asked Lee what brought her to the meeting.

Lee said that while she was fully engaged in life now, in a couple of months, she expected to be gone. Recently, she had said goodbye to her dentist, whom she knew she would not see again. She said she felt that she was in a chrysalis stage between a caterpillar and a butterfly, and that balancing between the two worlds felt odd, in some ways uncomfortable.

In other ways, it was comforting. Word about her plan was getting around the Unitarian Society, prompting conversations she wouldn't have had if her death were left up to chance. She said she liked the opportunity to consciously say goodbye. She also wanted no element of deception with her death, as sometimes happens with suicide.

"It's the sweetness of this kind of dying that I like," she

said. "It is so lovely to begin to have deep conversations and communication with people you know in a different way." Her daughter Sue asked about the timing — how did Lee know now was the right time, as opposed to last year or even a year from now?

Lee said it wasn't easy to actually pick a date to start the process. "I don't know that tomorrow will be a good day or even what makes a good day," she said. The one thing she was certain of was that she wanted her children around her when she died. "They are the most important people in my life," she said. "It's not going to be easy for me to leave them, and for them to leave me." But how did she know she was ready, someone asked.

"I'm more ready now than I would have been a couple weeks ago," she said. Lee offered a glimpse of how her life had changed, saying she felt fortunate to be lucid, but that everything was a tremendous effort. Tasks that once took an hour — like making soup stock — now stretched over several days. Her refrigerator was starting to feel like a dangerous place because to open the door, she had to let go of her walker to grab onto the handle. With that, she risked losing her balance, falling backwards, and needing to summon the EMTs.

Here, Zesiger stepped in to guide the conversation. "Lee," he said kindly, "I want to ask you how you're feeling."

He went through a checklist. How was her eating? She said she had no appetite and it was a chore to finish breakfast. Was she in pain? Lee reported that she was in pain pretty much all the time, especially after she'd been in one position for an extended period, which meant pain often interrupted her sleep. All her joints hurt. Her mobility issues had impacted her social life — she used to walk up to Lathrop's meetinghouse, and no longer could do that. How was her sleeping? She tended to sleep a few hours a night until the pain awakened her, she said. Consequently, it was hard to feel rested, so she fell asleep multiple times over the course of a day, including once while holding a cup of hot tea.

She reported no nausea, shortness of breath, depression or anxiety.

These details emerged only when Zesiger asked specifically and directly. Lee believed complaining made things worse. When Zesiger asked her to size up all her symptoms and her life to rate her general sense of well-being, she said: "Great."

But after Zesiger's gentle probing, it was clear to everyone in the room that Lee had chosen this summer to die because physically, she was ready. In a certain way, she'd had her fill, though she wouldn't put it that way, because that might seem like complaining.

She acknowledged that a partial answer to the "Why now?" question was that she finally had reluctantly accepted she should no longer live alone. The time to act is now, she said, simply because "I still can." Lee asked Zesiger to describe what death by stopping eating and drinking would be like. He said it would take about two weeks, possibly less, and that stopping drinking would be the key. After a few days, she would not feel hungry, but feeling thirsty would be challenging. She could be comforted by keeping her mouth moistened with a wet sponge on a stick. After several days she would likely sleep most of the time. In the second week she might summon enough energy for a special visit but would generally wake up for only a half an hour at a time.

Pain medication would help keep her comfortable but would not hasten or prolong the process. She would need care and companionship 24/7. Hospice could provide, or the family could hire, professional caregivers for daily living and medical needs, while family and friends would be present for comfort and companionship.

Zesiger turned his attention to Lee's daughters, asking them how they were feeling about their mother's plan. Both said they wanted to support their mother's wishes, but worried that with the wheels in motion, Lee might not feel she could change her mind if she had a change of heart.

Becky noted that her mother had always valued independence, choice and feeling in control of her life — and she'd never liked having things done for her. She could support Lee because she knew this was what her mother wanted, but it was painful, though she didn't want to talk much about that for fear it would make things harder for Lee. One other thing: If her mother complained of being thirsty and asked for water, she said, fighting back tears, "I don't think I could withhold it." Sue said she knew that no matter how well planned her mother's death was, there would be sadness and grieving. Yet she acknowledged that her mother's quality of life had diminished greatly. She said she did not think what Lee wanted to do was unreasonable.

Zesiger suggested they look at this like taking a car ride, and that at any point on the ride, they could choose to take a break and get off the road. Lee would be in charge, and if one day she asked for water or juice — or champagne, for that matter — they should feel free to give it to her. She could change her mind at any point. Zesiger told them that no matter how much planning they did, there would always be elements of uncertainty and factors beyond anyone's control.

"I don't think this has to be perfectly done because there's nothing perfect about this," said the physician.

He said Lee qualified for hospice care because in his

medical opinion she wouldn't live beyond six months even if she continued to eat and drink.

This declaration ushered in a new chapter in Lee Hawkins' life. Zesiger gave them all homework. Sue and Becky were to make an appointment with a hospice social worker. Lee should start thinking about where she wanted to die.

Lee makes a plan[*]

LEE HAWKINS NEVER HAD A BUCKET LIST. She felt she'd been living life the way she wanted. But in the weeks before she would undertake her plan to bring about her death by not taking in food or water, there were still some simple pleasures to indulge.

Her friend Janet Spongberg brought her to Puffer's Pond in Amherst, which she'd always wanted to see. Her daughter Becky brought her to Friendly's for lunch, something she and her late husband, Roger, had enjoyed. Her son, Jerry, picked up Lee's best friend, Grace, from her summer cottage in Sturbridge, driving her back to Lee's Northampton home to spend the night so the two friends could visit.

There were other items on her list, including updating her will, calling out-of-town friends to say goodbye, writing letters her children would read after she died. As for figuring out what to do with her cat, Bapu, she left that decision to her children.

On July 14, Lee and daughters Sue and Becky met with

[*] *Reprinted from the* Daily Hampshire Gazette, *September 24, 2014*

From left: Becky, Lee and Sue Hawkins, Sue's husband Wayne and Jerry Hawkins enjoy a meal together — one of the last Lee would eat before she stopped eating and drinking in August of 2014.

Dr. Zesiger a second time. Once again, when the physician asked Lee to rate her general sense of well-being, she said "10." But when pressed for details, she said though she could get to sleep, she always awoke in discomfort and pain. She tried taking morphine drops, but they provided no relief.

By this meeting, two weeks after their first, Lee had already begun receiving hospice services. Signing up with VNA & Hospice of Cooley Dickinson brought forth a team of helpers: A chaplain sat with her and played guitar. Nurses came to take her vital signs and make sure she was comfortable. A social worker came to sit and talk. An occupational therapist looked for ways to make the shower safer. Movers delivered a hospital bed and an automated chair that slowly moved until it had tipped Lee all the way up to standing, and later took her back to a reclining position.

Zesiger reported that he'd spoken with her primary care doctor, who was well acquainted with Lee's ideas. Over the years, she had informed him that if the time seemed right, she might undertake what she termed a "planned death."

Zesiger told Lee that he'd met with the Cooley Dickinson Hospital ethics committee, which had discussed Lee's case vigorously. Some members voiced objections and concerns. They had questions for Zesiger to bring back to her: Was she depressed? Would she be willing to see a psychiatrist to check out her emotional health? Lee said she was not depressed in the least, but that she would be willing to see a psychiatrist.

What about Lee's son, Jerry, whom Zesiger hadn't met — was he on board with his mother's plan, or might he later object? Lee and her daughters assured Zesiger that Jerry, like his sisters, believed wholeheartedly that Lee had the right to make this choice.

Did she have any religious beliefs that might conflict with her plans? No, Lee said. While she regularly attended church, Lee did not believe in an afterlife — or that God would disapprove of her plan.

The ethics team wondered about Lee's diminishing ability to care for herself. They asked if she might scrap her plans to end her life if she was matched up with help — specifically a chimpanzee trained to help disabled people. At this question, Lee and her daughters laughed uproariously, and Lee spit out, "If you give me a chimpanzee, I might change my mind!"

Dr. Jeffrey Zesiger, Lee's hospice doctor, hugs Lee after a meeting in August of 2014.

Later, Zesiger would say that this was actually a serious proposal, although nobody really thought Lee would want to pursue it. If she had, they would have had to get busy with some research.

In all seriousness, though, Lee had been starting to worry over the previous two weeks about whether she was safe alone in her home. "I just wonder if I can last through the next month and a half to be able to live the way I am now," she said.

Zesiger agreed. "My impression is your joints and your muscles are failing you," he said.

"Me too," Lee said emphatically.

Her daughters said they believed the time had come for Lee to stay out of the kitchen. While all three Hawkins children were prepared to be with their mother full time during the dying process, they were not able yet to leave their lives entirely — they had jobs to take leave from, gardens and pets to make arrangements for, projects to wind down for an extended stay away. A call went out to Lee's friends at the Unitarian Society requesting dinners so she would no longer need to cook. Already, a helper hired from Lathrop was making her breakfast, and they felt the helper could also set out lunch.

Circling back to the question of Lee's mental state, Zesiger said that Lee could meet with a hospice social worker in lieu of the requested session with a psychiatrist.

Zesiger said it seemed time to call on hospice services to help the family with some of the practical problems they faced, like bringing the occupational therapist in for a safety assessment. As for where she might die, Lee said she'd been thinking she might want to go to the Fisher Home, an inpatient hospice facility in Amherst, believing that might make it easier for everyone involved. Zesiger said that was her choice, and that she could use the CDH Hospice services at her home until she opted to go to the Fisher Home.

Zesiger wrapped up the meeting by saying now was the time to line up as much help as possible for Lee, with the goal of keeping her safe en route to the kind of death she envisioned.

With this, he held two hands up with crossed fingers. "With all alacrity, this is the week for making lots of plans," he said. He suggested Lee might even now set a date for when she intended to stop eating and drinking. Zesiger said goodbye to Lee, Becky and Sue, saying he might not see them again. They were in hospice care now, he said, and would require his help only if they needed to consult. He hugged each of them.

Within a matter of days, Lee's friends from the Unitarian Society had signed up to bring her meals through early August, when her children planned to come to stay. She had decided it would be somewhere around then that she would stop eating and drinking.

Meanwhile, word of Lee's plans had begun to get around enough so that regularly at Sunday services, friends approached her to say goodbye. The goodbyes picked up steam with the meal train. When people brought her dinners, they stayed to visit, and Lee, always a social person, loved these conversations.

Toward the end of July, she began mulling the idea of hosting a social gathering. It would be a time to visit with friends, a chance for them to ask any questions they had.

Her daughters had mixed feelings. They worried people might feel uncomfortable, and hadn't she been saying goodbye to people already? Their mother was a teacher at heart — was this a way to offer a teaching moment about a matter she held strong feelings about?

But for Lee, it was simpler than that. She just liked being with people she cared about. In the end, Lee decided to host an ice cream social, inviting a moderate number, leaving out her closest friends and others with whom she'd had time already. She hoped nobody felt left out.

On August 2, Lee sat on the brown leather recliner hospice movers had delivered to her living room. She wore a purple ribbed turtleneck — even in summer, she was always cold — black pants, matching silver earrings and necklace, comfortable shoes. She was sucking hard candy purchased by her son. Though she hadn't yet stopped eating and drinking, she was experiencing severe dry mouth, to the point that her lips would get stuck on her teeth. She found out that as people age, salivary glands can slow down. Water didn't help much, it turned out, but hard candy tended to activate the salivary glands and bring some relief.

Sue was away on business, but Becky and Jerry were there for the party. They spread fixings for root beer floats — Lee's favorite — and ice cream sundaes out on the table. Lee sat in her recliner as people took turns sitting on either side of her. Over the course of three hours, about twenty visitors stopped by, their arrivals spaced out to allow Lee to have quiet conversations with one or two at a time. One of those conversations was with a longtime friend, Addison Cate, who was ninety-four. They sat together, heads nearly touching, holding hands while they talked.

Jon Sass, a retired public school teacher who had become closer with Lee after Roger's death, was there as well, along with his wife, Christine. Jon and Lee had worked together on various committees and shared an abiding love for the Unitarian Society, where both felt they'd found kindred spirits. From time to time, the two of them had discussed Lee's ideas about death and ending her life.

The gathering that afternoon at Lee's home felt to Jon like a celebration of life that's usually held after someone has died. "It was joyous," he said. "But it was bittersweet, too." He was struck, he would later say, by Lee's bravery. "It's pretty profound to have someone make that decision when they're not at death's door. Lee chose to do it in a very thoughtful, deliberate manner and that was remarkable."

At the party, the mood was upbeat, and, it turned out, everything Lee hoped it would be. The next day, she talked about the difficulty of letting go of a life she had thoroughly enjoyed — and one she was enjoying still. "I have an article

I'm reading in *The New Yorker* and I say I can't die before I read it all because I need to know how it ends," she said. And then she laughed and added: "And I'm a slow reader!"

She reflected on the time she had recently been spending with people. She liked the deliberate way she was going about this business of dying.

"The conversations have been wonderful and I think what I would have missed — a lot of us say 'I wish I could die in my sleep,' but I would have missed so much," she said. Lee put her two hands together, linked by her fingers, and said this is what she felt like — beyond the caterpillar, in the chrysalis, not yet a butterfly. It's a funny place to be, she said.

Once an avid daily watcher of the *PBS NewsHour* and a woman who read the *Gazette* front to back, Lee had begun to pull away from the news. She wasn't sure if it was because hearing was so difficult, because reading was getting harder, or possibly that she was starting to lose interest in this world. It was a little freeing, she said. For so long, she had felt a great sense of responsibility to help try to fix the problems of the world.

"I'm shedding all responsibility, giving it all to you," she told me.

By this point, Lee and her daughters had decided she would not go to the Fisher Home, feeling it would be most comfortable to remain at home. There, her children could take up residence, helping her as needed, visiting with her and spelling each other when they needed breaks.

A few days after the ice cream social, Lee told her daughters she thought she'd stop eating and drinking on Monday, August 11. Then she received a telephone call from a teenage friend, a young woman who'd moved out of the area but remained attached to Lee. She wanted to visit but couldn't make it until Tuesday, August 12. At that point, Lee had decided she would have no more visitors once she'd stopped taking nourishment, so she told her young friend a visit wouldn't work out unless she could come sooner. When the girl told her she could not, Lee decided to push the date back.

"I am a procrastinator," she said later.

A couple of other matters cropped up that week to delay Lee's plans. Her grandchildren visited, prompting a final family dinner August 15 — certainly worth waiting for. She had a small matter in her will she wanted to change, so she made an appointment with her lawyer.

Meanwhile, the goodbyes unfolded. The morning helper who came most frequently had recently said: "I just want to tell you that you have changed for the good my thinking about life and death." Lee continued to say she was not frightened by what was ahead. When she said goodbye to friends, she did not say she would miss them, because that did not feel true. What she said was this: "I hope that in your memories I will have a warm spot because that's how I'll be here, in anything you will remember of me," she said. "What people remember of me is my afterlife."

Despite the delays in her decision, there were signs the time was coming near. She finished the *New Yorker* article she'd been reading and decided not to start another.

Accepting Lee's choice

WHILE LEE FOCUSED ON DECIDING WHERE TO DIE, tying up loose ends and saying goodbye, many of the people around her had reactions. Some struggled with her choice.

The Rev. Janet Bush watched as Lee's decision rippled among her many friends within the congregation. Some worried, fearing Lee would suffer. Others were perplexed: Why was she making what they saw as a private act into something so public?

Mostly though, "I think people respected her process," Janet said.

Barbara Smith, who had known Lee and Roger for years, had a deep respect for Lee, but was deeply disturbed by her friend's plans.

When she learned Lee was about to stop eating and drinking, Barbara had an immediate, strong reaction, though she kept it to herself at the time.

"I was pissed at her," she later recalled. "I loved being around Lee." Having enjoyed so many years of a friendship knit together by spontaneous visits to Lee and Roger's home to talk or pass an occasional evening playing games, Barbara couldn't see Lee as finished with life.

"I thought there was a lot more in her, a lot more vim and vigor," she said. "I thought she was checking out too early."

Lee's longtime friend Janet Spongberg also was troubled. She, too, worried that her friend's decision was premature. She couldn't help but wonder if it somehow represented a failure on the part of her community to support her more.

"If the village could have shown up ..." she said, a bit wistfully one day.

Janet also believed Lee's friendships contributed to her longevity.

"Having friends and being social was so profoundly life-giving that it literally kept her alive," she said.

Sue Hawkins wondered if her mother was truly ready to leave the friendships and connections she so clearly loved. She'd noticed, she said, how delighted her mother was when the UU-led meal train volunteers began stopping by, after the decision was made that Lee could no longer cook for herself.

"She could have cared less about the food — she wanted the company," said Sue. "She may have been lonelier than she admitted to."

Friends found it unnerving, even confusing, that Lee was so obviously engaged with life even as she prepared to leave it of her own volition. Patricia Wright, whose friendship with Lee began just a few years before she died, was surprised at how interested Lee was in learning more details about Patricia's life. Lee still wanted more, even as her body weakened in the days after she ceased eating and drinking.

"I don't think I've got a clear idea how your family got from Nebraska to Los Angeles," Lee said one day, as Patricia sat with her. And then, Lee asked her to explain.

Janet Bush observed Lee several times push back the day she would activate her plan.

"She was very clear and she was very determined," the minister said. "And yet she was still finding things in life to enjoy and appreciate. Life is a gift."

Like others in Lee's circle, Cathy Lilly was well aware of Lee's strong feelings about the resources devoted to medical care at the end of long lives.

"She took a very strong stance as she got closer to her decline and I somewhat disagreed with her," Cathy said. "It was very consistent with so many other things she believed."

Cathy and her husband, Bill Whitehill, struck up a friendship with Lee and Roger after they began attending the Unitarian Society in 1992 and became close in a long-running monthly dinner group.

But Cathy also understood that Lee wanted to remain

independent — and that she was facing her decline without her spouse. She recalled a weekend years earlier when Roger and Lee invited friends to visit them at their cottage in Sturbridge. The cottage was up on a bluff overlooking the lake, with a steep staircase down to the water. Roger could no longer make it to the beach on his own steam. His friends carried him down the steps so they could enjoy the water together, like old times. When it was time to leave, they carried him back up.

Lee with Rev. Janet Bush, minister of the Unitarian Society of Northampton and Florence, where Lee was a member for many years.

Lee never would have gone for that, Cathy said: That was one of the differences between them. At the end of his life, Roger did not mind accepting a little help; for Lee, independence was paramount.

"He declined in a very natural way with help at home and was able to participate in anything he wanted to with Lee's help," Cathy said. "She had decisions to make, and those were never questions for Roger."

Lee's friend Heather Johnson had witnessed the hazards living on her own posed for Lee as she became weaker. The two women's friendship had been kindled in the years after Roger died when they discovered they shared a passion for politics and current events. They would watch *60 Minutes* on Sundays and *Washington Week* and the *PBS NewsHour* on Fridays, and then stay up late discussing what it all meant.

"It was like being in college, you know, you just don't have those kinds of talks anymore. It was just great," she said.

But Heather noticed the toll aging was taking. They'd have to turn the television up earsplittingly loud, and Lee still needed the closed captioning. However, she couldn't read the captions fast enough, and this was equally frustrating.

On more than one occasion when Heather was visiting, Lee fell. She couldn't get up on her own, nor could Heather hoist her up. So they'd summon help and then wait together, chatting the whole time.

"We'd have discussions where we were both sitting on the floor," Heather recalled. "I couldn't lift her up, so we would just keep going."

As it happened, Lee and Heather lost touch in the year or so before Lee died. Four nights before she discontinued nourishment, Lee, her daughters, Janet, Patricia and I were at the kitchen table chatting over root beer floats when Heather stopped by with a piece of fancy chocolate cake she thought Lee would enjoy.

As the visit unfolded, it seemed that Heather was piecing together the fact that Lee was preparing to bring about her death.

Later, Heather would say that realization had been devastating. She held it together, but once out in her car alone in the dark, she sobbed. "I was a wreck," she said. "I was blown away because, you know, you always think it's going to be at some point in the distant future."

My own friendship with Lee at that time was still young, but it had covered intimate territory that made it go deep quickly. With both her words and her actions, Lee let me see just how important it was to do things for herself as long as she could. I often gave her rides to and from services on Sundays. When I sat next to her in the pews, I could never seem to stop myself from trying to help her with the heavy hymnals when it came time to sing. To me, it seemed she had enough to do just pulling herself up to standing, let alone dealing with the hymnal and opening it to the right page. But she would never let me help. She didn't want me to hand it to her, open it for her, or hold it for her.

Still, I kept showing up, learning from her the simple gift of being present. I vowed to myself to try to tell her as honestly as I could what I was feeling as long as it wouldn't burden her.

One day, I had a strong urge to hold her hand, but we'd never done that so I felt awkward. So that's exactly what I told her.

"Oh, I would love that," she said.

That was when we started holding hands.

Lee's goodbye[*]

EARLY IN AUGUST, Becky hung a dry-erase board on a wall in her mother's home and their days started to take shape around it. Becky, Sue or Jerry would jot down plans for the day, the next day, or a few days out, reminders about recycling or trash pickup, upcoming visits from friends, appointments with the hospice nurse, social worker or appointments outside the house, like the one with Lee's lawyer. In between events noted in red and blue marker on the whiteboard, the Hawkins children and their mother played games, read books, watched movies, and talked. On the board for Wednesday, August 13, were these words: HOSPICE POWWOW 2:45.

By 2:30 on August 13, the daughters had made a circle of chairs in the living room, taken some cookies from the oven, set a pot of Earl Grey tea to steep. Around 2:45, team members arrived, greeting and hugging Lee. She sat comfortably in a leather reclining chair with ten people circled around her, Dr. Zesiger among them. At their last meeting, he'd said he likely wouldn't see them all again, but as Lee's case made

[*] *Reprinted from the* Daily Hampshire Gazette, *September 25, 2014*

its way up the chain of command at the VNA & Hospice of Cooley Dickinson, agency leaders had taken steps to develop new protocols.

Zesiger opened the meeting by explaining that Lee's case was unusual. For the hospice team, her decision had prompted a consultation with a hospice ethicist, many meetings, and a new protocol. They wanted Lee to sign a two-page form describing the process Cooley Dickinson Hospice would follow when receiving requests from patients to voluntarily stop eating and drinking. This included evaluating each patient's ability to make an informed decision, and a determination that they were not depressed. The form also noted that any hospice staff could opt out of caring for a patient choosing to die in this manner.

Lee didn't question the form, signing it without complaint. Then she asked Zesiger to go over once again what she should expect when she stopped eating and drinking.

"People who stop eating and drinking one hundred percent don't live past two weeks," he said. "The first couple of days you could feel hunger, but the hunger goes away pretty quick. Drinking and thirst is usually the thorniest problem."

Lee admitted to some worry about what it would be like to not drink at all, and the team discussed strategy to deal with uncomfortable symptoms: swabbing the mouth with water, sucking on ice chips, keeping her lips well moisturized with lip balm. Lee said her son discovered a technique she'd already found helpful: sucking on hard candy to activate her slowed-down salivary glands.

Zesiger described how her energy would diminish. She would become weaker, spend more time in bed, more time sleeping and less time chatting.

"I wouldn't expect there'll be any pain, any trouble breathing, any upset stomach," said Zesiger. If there were any pain or agitation, he said, medicine could help with that discomfort.

Lee replied, "So, it sounds like there's not much to worry about."

They touched on the matter of timing. Lee had previously set a date to cease food and water, only to push it back when events came up for which she wanted to be present. At this point she was expecting it would be soon, but was taking it day by day. She said she found it hard to set a date when she was so engaged in meaningful connections with many of her friends. But things were starting to feel different, Lee said — and her daughters agreed. There were fewer visitors, the house more quiet. Lee had stopped attending Sunday services.

"Everything that's important, I think, has passed," she

Lee and her daughter, Sue

said. She noted that she had been eating very little because she had no appetite.

"With you already eating and drinking less, it's clear to me that you're on the end of your life road," said Zesiger.

He explained that the team had decided after all to ask Lee to see a psychiatrist, to consult with a professional who could be sure that she was not depressed.

"You're sort of pushing the envelope on what people do," he told her. "I don't believe you have depression that's guiding your wish to die; I don't think you are fuzzy in the head at all."

But an appointment with a psychiatrist would make all that clear.

"This is new territory and we're building something," he said. And there are people, he told Lee, who would adamantly oppose what she was doing. Lee responded that she knew that, but wanted to clarify if what she was about to embark upon was legal. It was absolutely her right, he told her, to stop eating and drinking.

Zesiger said he'd reached out to a psychiatrist who could see Lee the following week.

Lee was game, but all three children objected. Jerry said they all knew Lee was not depressed, and a visit with a psychiatrist seemed an unnecessary hoop.

"It's the end of her life and I would like to see her do it the way she wants, not the way I want, not the way you want," said Jerry. Her daughters felt Lee had already been acutely sensitive to other people's needs, and she would again put off the process to accommodate others even when it might not be in her best interest. One noted that they'd enrolled with hospice in June; it seemed late in the game to ask for this, pretty much on the eve of her plan to stop eating and drinking.

"I just really want Mom to make the decision internally, not externally," said Sue.

In the end, Zesiger said he would ask the psychiatrist if he could see Lee sooner. The team agreed that Lee should go about her plan as she wished, and if she became too weak to make the appointment, they could cancel.

"I hope you all feel that what you are doing is to honor your mom's wishes and walk this road with her," said Maureen Groden, hospice and palliative care manager for CDH. "It is honorable." She reminded them that hospice team members could answer more questions, and that among the services available were a music program and a harp program which many dying people and their families found comforting.

Lee looked small in her oversized chair. "Thank you all for coming and taking good care of me," she said. "It really is such a great comfort to have both family and hospice." The meeting broke up after ninety minutes, again with a lot of hugging as the hospice team said goodbye to Lee one by one.

Afterwards, Lee confessed that she was harboring another worry about what was to come.

"I may get nasty. Sometimes you have a personality change," she said. "I just hope I don't turn against my kids."

The next day, Zesiger called to say he had managed to get Lee an appointment with a psychiatrist that afternoon.

Becky drove her mother to Amherst, where the psychiatrist asked her questions and in short order pronounced that Lee was neither depressed nor being coerced — and that she was most definitely of sound mind.

On August 14, four days before Lee Hawkins stopped eating, she sat in her wheelchair at her dining-room table along with her daughters and four friends from the Unitarian Society enjoying root-beer floats. The conversation was light, friends chatting on a summer night.

Lee described a bike trip she'd taken in Italy in her twenties, when she'd failed to bring enough water along. Everyone laughed as she described how when she stopped at a restaurant seeking water, they kept trying to give her wine, and she kept insisting all she wanted was water. Others described their misadventures on trips in their twenties. There were indications that Lee was her usual sharp-as-a-tack self, as when someone mentioned suffering a 105-degree fever, and she said adamantly, "It could not have been a 105 fever."

But there were other signs that the conversation was hard for her, either due to her hearing issues, or because she was experiencing confusion, as when she interrupted during one story to say, "What are you talking about now?"

During this time, there was some discussion about what would happen to her cat Bapu, who was regularly around Lee when she was in her recliner or in bed, after Lee died. Her children loved the cat, but couldn't take him, so in the end it was decided Bapu would go to friends from church.

The following Monday, Lee said she didn't feel like eating. The next day, her children sat at the dining room table eating a roast chicken dinner while Lee sat nearby in her recliner, chatting with them. She teased them playfully about making a meal she would have enjoyed. In fact, they gave her a bite, pretty much all she wanted. That was the last food she would ever eat. She stopped drinking two days after that.

※

So began a period when one day seemed like several days. Life for the Hawkins clan took on a timeless quality. Becky, Sue and Jerry used a monitor to listen in on Lee when they were not in the room with her, and at night when they slept. They gave her morphine regularly, and pills to calm agitation or anxiety when she needed them.

Earlier, Sue had asked Lee to choose a book they could read to her. She suggested it be a book Lee was familiar with so if she was drifting in and out, she would still get the gist of the story. Lee chose *Heidi,* and while many people read it to her, Becky did so most often, reading to Lee for stretches at a time, whether she was awake or not. Jerry brought out his guitar to play and sing to Lee. Sue read from books of poetry, including the work of Rumi and Maya Angelou, which she'd checked out of the Forbes Library.

There were vases of flowers everywhere. Lee loved them, and when friends stopped by, most had a small bunch in hand. Everyone knew Lee didn't like "showy" flowers, so the bouquets were small enough to fit on the crowded table next to her bed or on the bookshelf she could see from the bed. Most days a few friends stopped by, holding Lee's hand, singing or reading quietly even when Lee could not be roused. Hospice staff came regularly, sometimes giving Lee sponge baths, which she slept through.

Lee's appearance began to change. Her face shrunk inward, her wedding ring and diamond grew so loose that they twirled around on her finger and looked as if they might fall off. But her spirits continued to be upbeat. She would wake up with a smile on her face, asking who was in the house and what everyone was up to. She sometimes awoke laughing, as if she'd just had a good dream.

Lee liked having her face spritzed with rose water, and when her children asked her if she'd like it, she would often say with quiet enthusiasm: "Always." The thirst was difficult for everyone. Her children gave her lozenges made to relieve dry mouth, and glycerin squirts that provided some relief. When that bottle ran out, they filled it with water and squirted her dry mouth with a few spritzes. One day, Lee held her hand out and made a small circle with her thumb and index finger.

"Before I die, I want this much root beer," she said, smiling mischievously. When Becky asked Lee if she wanted the root beer right then, Lee said maybe later.

Another day, she said she wished Zesiger and Andrée LeBlanc-Ross, her nurse, could tell her precisely when she would die, so that just the moment before she died, she could have a large glass of water.

One day her granddaughter surprised her with a visit, with her young daughter and a friend, so two children were in the house, which made Lee happy. "It's kind of nice to end your life around a lot of people who are starting theirs," she said, a little dreamily.

Later she recalled that many years ago, when she first moved to Lathrop, she had neighbors who frequently entertained their grandchildren, and she loved hearing the children play outside. "I think we should write a note and put it in the Lathrop newsletter that that was my happiest time at Lathrop," she said quietly.

Lee was alternately lucid or engaged in periods of sharing

stream-of-consciousness thoughts about her childhood, her parents, and her father's courtship of her mother. One day she told a visitor with some urgency that there were so many different parts to her life, but she was the only person who knew them all. Perhaps, she said, somebody should write them all down. And suddenly she blurted out: "I have a thought!" She told Becky she needed to write a note to her grandson's girlfriend to tell her how much she appreciated her. Later she announced: "I have decided that *Heidi* is the source of all my values."

On a warm late August day without a cloud in the sky, Lee was sitting up in bed listening to Becky read from *Heidi*. Every once in a while she asked a question about what she'd heard, as in "was that 'coffee' or 'toffee?'" Out the window she noticed Jerry returning from a walk in the woods with his two pit bulls, Ruckus and Caina, bringing a smile to her face. When Becky finished the chapter, Lee asked to be taken outside, and so Becky helped her mom into a sweater, socks and slippers. With help from a visitor and the automatic hospital bed, she managed to get her severely weakened mother into the wheelchair and outside, where Lee asked to be wheeled to a spot in the sun with a view of her flower beds.

That she was strong enough to sit up in her wheelchair to enjoy the summer day a week after she'd had her last meal surprised everyone. Becky and Jerry sat on the grass next to Lee; the dogs flopped down, panting from their run in the woods. They must remain outside at least until Sue, who had been running errands, returned, said Becky. "Sue will want to see this."

On several days when Lee slept most of the day, she awoke with renewed energy in the early evening. One of these evenings she sat in her recliner while Sue and Becky pulled pictures from a box and reminisced about their childhood: Camp Fire Girls appearances in the town parade, Lee's elaborate birthday cakes and the way they were coordinated with the activity of the party, like the time she made a turtle-shaped cake when they'd gone to the Turtle Back Zoo in New Jersey. The daughters told stories. Lee, weak, tired, and hoarse from not drinking, chimed in with small additions, questions, or corrections. They each had a glass of wine, and Lee asked for some, surprising her daughters because she was not a wine-drinker. With Becky's help, Lee took a sip and said that was enough.

The next day, Lee was too weak to get out of bed at all, and the day after that, she didn't wake up. Her children and her friends continued to sit by her side reading, singing, talking, holding her hands and stroking her hair. She received several Reiki treatments, provided by hospice, which her children thought helped keep Lee calm and comfortable. On September 1, Becky finished reading *Heidi* while Lee was receiving Reiki.

On the morning of September 2, feeling the end was near, Sue arranged for the harpist to come play. Around five P.M., Sue and Becky sat on either side of Lee's bed holding her hands, while Jerry stood at the top of the bed, stroking Lee's face. They felt Lee had signaled without words an awareness that the harpist was in the room as she set her instrument up at the foot of the bed, and began playing. Soon, Sue realized Lee had stopped breathing. Then Becky noticed. Sue let Jerry know. When the harpist stopped for a moment to tune the instrument, Sue whispered to her that Lee had died. The harpist asked if she should keep playing, Sue nodded, and they continued sitting with Lee as harp music played.

After the harpist left, Sue and Becky dressed Lee in a pair of light green corduroy pants, a summery flowered top, and her favorite, wildly striped socks. They combed her hair and put on a pair of earrings.

"What a good, used-up body she has," Sue said, as she and her siblings lingered with their mother.

The children agreed that the most difficult part of the past weeks had been the final three days when Lee was unconscious and they could not find out from her what she needed.

"It was awful when she couldn't communicate," said Jerry.

"What death isn't hard?" said Sue. "I feel like she was really, really uncomfortable, but I don't think she was really suffering."

The next day, the crematorium would come to pick up Lee's body. Hospice movers would arrive to take away the hospital bed and reclining chair. Sue, Becky and Jerry would meet again with the hospice social worker.

But for that moment, music quietly played and three children sat with their mother, vases of flowers all around. No words were needed.

After Lee

AFTER LEE'S CHILDREN CLEARED OUT HER HOME at the end of Golden Chain Lane, Sue and Becky continued to visit Northampton, maintaining connections with many people they'd met through their parents. They still occasionally joined their mother's dinner group, where they also became friends with their parents' close friends, Cathy and Bill. After Lee died, they asked the couple to take in Lee's cat, Bapu.

These friendships included a small group of women — Janet Spongberg, Patricia Wright, Heather Johnson and me — who'd spent time with Lee at the end of her life. We gathered every few months, sharing memories about Lee and her unusual death while also keeping up on the changes in each other's lives.

In the way of silly nicknames, one emerged in our emails to plan get-togethers. It started as the Sisterhood of Lee Hawkins' Traveling Pants, then became Lee's Traveling Pants, then Lee's Pants. At some point, group email salutations became "Pants!"

In June 2018, four years after Lee died, I invited these

women and Lee's daughters, Sue and Becky, to dinner. I wanted to hear about how their experiences of Lee's death had changed over time.

"I never felt sad that she was making this decision," said Becky. "She had a great life. Do I think she could have continued having a great life? Maybe."

But in the next breath, Becky described a time she wrapped up a phone call with her mother.

"Love you, have a great day," Becky said.

"Ah, they're not great anymore," was Lee's reply.

Sue spoke of missing her mother, but also said she'd found the passing of time had eased the loss. There had been parts of that process that had been confusing and painful in ways not necessarily related to loss — disagreements with her mother, even difficulties in navigating her mother's indecision about the process. There is no rulebook and the Hawkins family was making it up, together, as they went along. But all of these stressors, she realized, were resolved.

"When I think back on it, I think, well, death isn't easy," she said. "The things that made it difficult and frustrating sort of faded."

As we lingered in the summer-night air on my back deck, Janet said time also had helped her come to terms with Lee's decision. She no longer sees it as a failure on the part of those around her to support her more.

"I understand her choice better now," she said. "I understand it, and I admire her clarity."

Each of us, it seemed, had found that over time, the clarity of Lee's decisions and our love for her ameliorated any reservations we might initially have harbored.

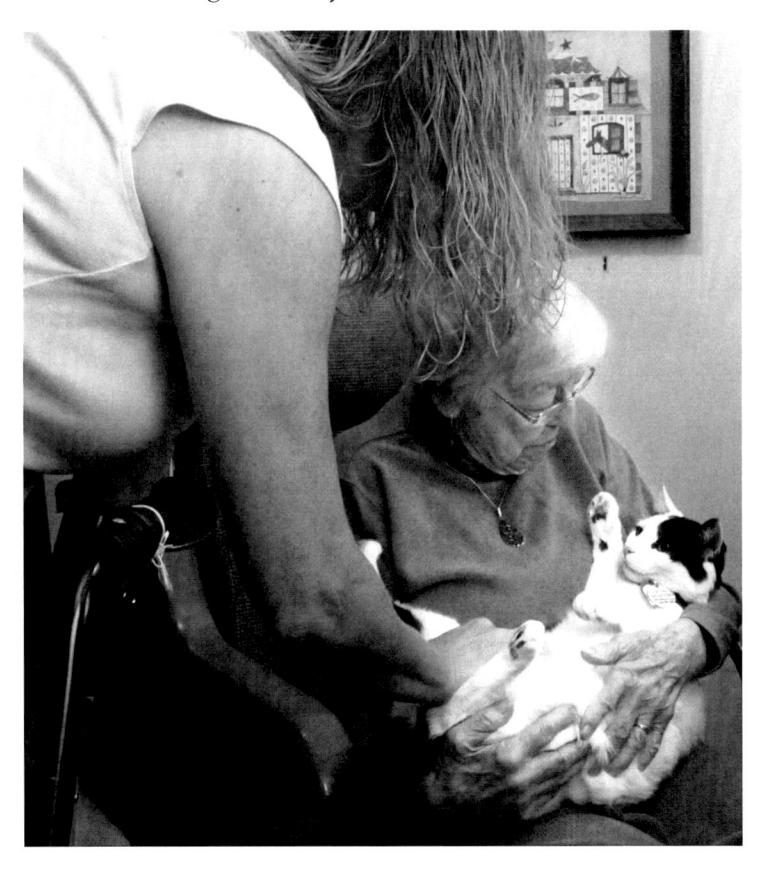

Becky Hawkins with Lee and Bapu, who was taken in by friends after Lee died.

"I wished she wasn't going to be gone, but she seemed so certain about it. I thought it was so brave," said Patricia.

Heather said she frequently thinks about Lee's methodical approach to her death.

"It was a whole new concept and it did open my eyes to other ways of planning for the end of your life," she said. "I admire her. It requires an immense amount of courage to see it through. I think it takes courage on the family's part and her part, because most people don't want to face that."

Meanwhile, other friends of Lee found their feelings evolved as well. Barbara Smith, who had felt angry about Lee's decision at the time, said her feelings about Lee's choices took a turn a year later when her own mother was dying in a dementia unit. During her many visits with her mother, Barbara gained a more nuanced understanding of the realities that had motivated Lee.

"I began to think differently about Lee's decision," she said. "I could definitely consider this for myself."

Cathy Lilly believes Lee's fearlessness helped her sort through her own thinking about how she might approach her final years and even prompted her to widen the scope of choices she might consider.

"I'm at the stage in my life where I'm sort of watching how people die," said Cathy, who is seventy-five. "I'm sort of getting clues about how different people do it."

Cathy's views evolved to the point where she understands more clearly why Lee made them.

"You don't have to do it in the way that your family did, or your religion dictates, or your upbringing suggests," she said. "I think this is the most important thing people my age can do. All those questions that you used to have as a young person are answered, so you settle on how you age and how you are going to die. Lee is a very good model."

Role model she may be, but that does not mean Cathy intends to follow in her friend's footsteps.

"I might not have checked out as early as she did," she said. "My goal is to live productively to be one hundred."

✳

The series about Lee, titled "Life, Death & Lee," ran in the *Daily Hampshire Gazette* September 23-25, 2014. The stories were displayed prominently, taking up much of the front page and substantial space inside the paper as well. They drew immediate, strong reaction from readers — both positive and negative. Calls came into the newsroom. Discussions about her death and the public nature of it played out for weeks afterwards on the *Gazette's* editorial page.

Some readers objected to Lee's decisions on religious and

moral grounds. Worse, they felt the paper's chronicling of her story was a tacit endorsement of her choice. Others were furious at the paper for publishing stories about something they felt was so deeply personal. Some felt the series had exploited Lee. Others called it sensational. A few readers argued it was in poor taste to publish pictures of someone wasting away; some were appalled the paper published a picture of a person immediately after death.

Photo editor Carol Lollis said there was never any question in her mind that the series needed to include a picture of Lee after death.

"The story was about Lee dying. I didn't think you could leave out the fact that she died," she said. "It would be like writing a story without the last paragraph in it."

She knew the family had trepidations and she respected that. She also knew photographs of people who are dead are disturbing to look at, so she had a fine line to walk.

"I knew I had to figure out a way to take a photo that honored the family and honored Lee and left her some dignity," she said. "A photo that evoked some emotion in the reader, but not repulsion."

As she spent time at Lee's apartment, she noticed a window off the front entrance that looked into Lee's study, where, as the end neared, the family had wheeled her hospital bed. She made a mental note that the window might be the view of Lee after death that met all those requirements.

After Lee died, Becky and Sue texted me. I called Carol immediately. She said she was on her way. It was dark when she arrived and as she looked into the study's window, she saw Lee in her bed. She took the photograph, then entered the house. As Becky, Sue and Jerry sat surrounding their mother talking about her death, she took another one.

There is one irony in Lee's death: For all her careful planning, she made no cremation arrangements. After Carol left that evening, I stayed on. I asked my partner, Lydia, to bring over some food for everyone. When she found out there had been no plans made, she suggested she could take on that task, an offer Jerry, Sue, and Becky happily accepted. Lydia called several funeral homes that quoted exorbitant prices; eventually she found a crematorium in Vermont, where the owners quoted half the price of the funeral homes that would have had to send Lee's body to a crematorium. They said they would be there first thing in the morning to pick up Lee's body. This gave Jerry, Sue and Becky one more night with their mother and the opportunity for a sweet goodbye in the morning.

※

The majority of people who called and wrote about the series admired Lee's openness and honesty, and thanked her — and the paper — for a story that put an often hidden, but important topic front and center. Other readers, hungry for information about end-of-life choices, thanked the paper for providing a starting point for their own thinking. Some letter-writers described agonizing decisions they had been forced to make as a loved one declined. These letters showed me that people want and need to talk freely about questions surrounding how to care for our aging friends and relatives now that so many of us are living substantially longer lives.

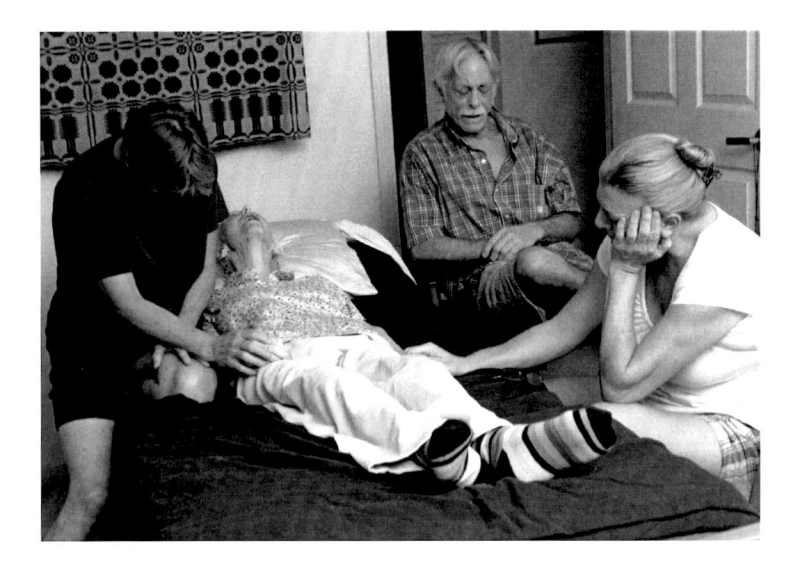

For many months after the series ran, Carol said people stopped her on assignments, on the streets, even in her car.

"I knew what was coming and I would brace myself, thinking 'Okay, which way is it going to go?' They were either going to yell at me or they were going to love it," she said. Those encounters, she said, continued much longer and more intensely than any other story she'd been involved in.

"I kept thinking, no matter what they say, we must have done a good thing because everybody has a feeling about it," she said.

From people within Lee's Unitarian congregation and readers of the newspaper, there were ongoing questions about why Lee chose to be so public about her process.

To me, her approach seemed straightforward and in keeping with who she was. Sure, she was a teacher, and there may have been part of her that wanted to educate people.

But I think there was something else. Lee valued community. She valued her independence. But when she really needed her community, she wanted it to be there for her. She expected it, and she was confident she could count on people to show up.

Lee let herself be vulnerable enough to ask for what she needed, which in the end was quite simple: She wanted her friends to stay close so she needn't approach death alone. And show up they did.

Scattering Paul's ashes

IN THE MONTHS FOLLOWING Lee's slow and peaceful death, I once again reviewed the circumstances leading up to my father's quick and violent death. Spending time with Lee and her children ultimately became a turning point for me in reaching a greater understanding of his actions.

Through Lee's eyes, I came to see how deeply my father struggled with his own aging-related limitations. I realized that I may have missed signs that he was at his personal tipping point, where he no longer wanted to try new things.

That understanding ultimately helped me take in the words my father wrote at his kitchen table the night he killed himself. "Tonight, I didn't mean to deceive you because I love you all much more than you realize," he had written.

"If I lost my mind, I'd regret that I let it happen to me, and I have to do what I feel is the correct thing for me to do," he'd written. "Try to understand it's a must for me to avoid future pain."

As Lee died, I witnessed the way she and her children navigated her death — imperfectly, tentatively, awkwardly, even messily at times, but always — always — lovingly. This experience helped me finally come to believe what she'd written in signing off the letter she'd typed in response to my column: "You have lost a warm, thoughtful, caring father."

✻

For all the differences in the way my father and Lee approached their deaths, what each wanted was personal choice. Free choice is a powerful human craving at any age. It's one often lost to people at the end of their lives.

I know Lee wasn't afraid of death because I asked her about that and her answer was resolute: She saw it as nothing to fear. I never asked my father, but I believe he, too, was unafraid of death.

He did have fears, though, and they centered around being trapped in a life that had become a shell of itself.

Not long before Dad died, we children chipped in to buy him an iPad. He'd taken computer literacy courses years prior and we saw that he appreciated the benefits of technology. He also loved the challenge of learning new things. We thought the iPad would widen his world at a time when his failing body was making it a more limited place.

He spent a lot of time trying to master it, with much

cursing in the process. In retrospect, I think it created more frustration than enjoyment.

I also recalled our time together early that last spring of his life when he and I helped Dan with chores to open up his camp for the season. These chores include a lot of literal heavy lifting. Though a tiny man, Dad was strong and a bit of a bulldog when it came to moving heavy objects. This time, though, he seemed excessively tired and not as strong as usual. He dropped something, causing a minor injury to his arm. He didn't talk about it, but he seemed deeply frustrated, even angry. At the time, I chalked it up to a bad mood.

These seem like small things, normal for people his age. I now believe he was at a point where learning and trying new things — always sources of excitement — had become instead sources of great frustration and irritation.

I probably shouldn't have been surprised. My father was usually in a hurry, never one to linger, often abrupt around goodbyes and transitions. He was famous in my family for taking down the Christmas tree on Christmas night. He walked quickly. He made decisions fast — some might say impulsively — and he could be impatient. I should not have been surprised that he could not linger with me the way I would have liked around one of the biggest transitions life puts in our path.

Maybe I just couldn't see that, to him, these were intolerable possibilities: help he didn't want, the confiscation of his checkbook, evaluations of his decisions, a feeling of being watched, infirmity, dependence, lack of mental clarity.

Being a reporter, I sought resolution the best way I know how, which is to look for answers. Four months after he died, I phoned his doctor at the VA hospital, who was kind and gracious and happy to answer my questions. No, he had not recently been given a troubling medical diagnosis. No, she did not think he was clinically depressed. Her feeling was that he simply made a rational choice that, to him, was the right thing to do. He had not told her of his plans for suicide, perhaps sensing — correctly — that she would have felt duty-bound to intervene.

But ultimately, she said she believed nobody had failed him, most definitely not his family. She said she had no judgement about what he did, and gently encouraged me, if I were harboring any lingering guilt, to let it go.

In retrospect I see that my cheerful attempts to suggest an alternate view of what was barreling down on him put distance between us, the way trying to fix things can. That human impulse to fix another person's life can be insidious in the way it separates us.

I still wish he'd seen more options, and that he'd chosen one of them. I do feel he took action much sooner than necessary. Who knows, maybe he could have gotten used to accepting help. That phase of life can bring a family to new levels of intimacy, as I witnessed with Lee's family.

And because my father's choice necessarily involved deception, it precluded the kind of conversations I believe would have provided comfort and resolution, both for him and his children.

Most of all, I wish that he did not feel he had to do this all alone. If Lee's death helped me understand my father's choices better, is also showed me that even in the midst of sorrow and anguish — in spite of the pain people inflict on each other intentionally and unintentionally — a person can remain connected to the people who love them. There is meaning in that connection.

As the Rev. Kate Braestrup, a Unitarian minister, offered as a guest on the podcast *Becoming Wise*: "The question isn't whether we're going to have to do hard, awful things, because we are — we all are. The question is whether we have to do them alone." I found solace in that idea, as I know Lee did. I wish my father could have, too.

When I think back to the note he left us, I know he tried so hard to soften the blow. He didn't imagine it would fall to the floor, that the police wouldn't find it, that we'd park the car for days and not go inside.

He did not imagine that sequence of events. He only thought police would come to our door, delivering the news and his note to us. The one in which he apologized for deceiving us, instructed us to love each other, to please understand this was a must for him, but above all else that he loved us more than we could know.

The note, coming as it did six days later, helped me understand him more: It told me that he couldn't live with himself if he lost his mind. I found it comforting, if only because I saw that he at least understood the impact on us of what he was about to do.

Paul on Messalonskee Lake in Belgrade, Maine, with Dan Loisel in the background.

Over time, I got answers to many of my questions, though others will remain unanswered. I'll never know exactly when my father decided to act. Had he already made up his mind when he said goodbye to us that night? Some of my siblings are convinced he had. Or did he decide as he drove home from dinner, thinking, "Why not now? What's left to say?"

I also don't know if he'd be alive today if he hadn't killed himself — just that he'd be ninety-one and the story I would tell about his death would be vastly different.

But time, distance and perspective change our stories even as we spin them.

Eight months after my father died, we gathered at my brother's camp on Messalonskee Lake, where we reminisced with family and friends. Then we children went out in Danny's boat to scatter our father's ashes in the lake. We didn't have a planned ritual. We didn't recite spiritual or healing words. We simply took turns letting the ashes fly into the breeze and watched them settle, then melt into the water. We knew that's where he'd want to be. That evening after dinner, someone put on music. Many of us danced. We all knew for sure Dad would have liked that.

Addenda

My family's decision to tell the truth about suicide

Published in the Daily Hampshire Gazette *April 25, 2013*

By Laurie Loisel, Staff Writer

NORTHAMPTON — On December 3, 2012, my father killed himself. He wasn't sick. He wasn't depressed. He wasn't impulsive. He drove to a police station parking lot, got out of his car and shot himself in the head with a hunting rifle he'd purchased a month before. He left in his car identification, documents with instructions about cremation, a copy of the do-not-resuscitate order he'd long kept on his refrigerator, and a note to his six children.

In the days following, my siblings and I found ourselves on an emotional battlefield battered by shock, sadness, fury, hurt, despair, confusion, and anguish.

We had to make many decisions together. One we were in complete agreement about was to be open about what he did. And for that, I am grateful; we didn't complicate an already horrible situation by pretending it was something it wasn't.

Two days after his suicide, we ran an obituary in my

hometown newspaper in Augusta, Maine, that started out like this: "Paul Reginald Loisel, 83, died Dec. 3 the way he lived his life — on his own terms. Paul spent a joyful evening having a belated Thanksgiving dinner with his family, during which time many stories were told and many laughs were shared. Later that night, Paul took his own life."

I know it is shocking to think that someone would share a seemingly lovely evening with his children, then say goodbye, and hours later kill himself in such a violent way. Trying to make sense of what my father did — both the fact that he did it and the way he did it — has made grieving the loss immeasurably harder.

When my mother died in June of 2011, I was at her bedside holding her hand. It was the sort of death you hope for when hospice gets involved: peaceful, expected, natural. Sad, yes, but somehow acceptable. (My parents had been divorced for over forty years, so her death had nothing to do with his decision.)

My father's death felt unnatural, unacceptable, violent and, in my heart, avoidable. He had, over the previous six months in conversations with several of us, let on that he considered suicide an alternative to an old age he feared might involve diminishment of his mental faculties. We engaged in these conversations, offering different ways to look at this, but all thought he was talking about a time way in the future when he might be too ill to continue on.

The weekend before he killed himself, sensing an actual plan was being formed, several of my siblings and I flew and drove home, circling the wagons in an attempt to put things in place to make him feel better about aging. We spent time with him, over lunch, brunch, dinner and tea. We took him to see *Lincoln*. We had many pointed conversations about old age, infirmity, dependency, a family's commitment to one another, and, yes, suicide.

He agreed there were many joyful things in his life. His children, for one, and our families. Books from the public library to rant and rave about (church scandals and atheism among his favorite topics), football games to watch and classes to take at the local community college. He was learning to use his new iPad.

But like a lawyer arguing a case, he said from his vantage point that old age seemed unbearable. He wanted to make his own bed, drive himself to the grocery store, make his own meals. He'd seen how others had suffered. The man across the hall had a stroke that left him debilitated. His sister-in-law hadn't recognized him on his last visit.

He was not depressed, he insisted when I gently inquired. But when he looked into what might be in his future, he wanted nothing to do with it.

Over dinner the night he killed himself, we again

explored many topics, among them aging, meaning of life and feelings about death. I told him I wanted to be with him when he died, as I had with my mother. After my father hugged us goodbye and left for his apartment, every one of us felt relieved, believing we'd had a successful intervention.

Several hours later, we were awakened by police banging on my sister's front door with the news that my father's body had been discovered in the police station parking lot.

We could not bring him around to our way of thinking. He preferred death over letting old age have its way with him.

It's not a choice I agree with, or even understand, really. I don't oppose this choice under all situations — I voted in favor of the physician-assisted suicide referendum that failed in our state last November. But in my view, my father still had vital years ahead of him.

It wasn't my choice to make, though, and I've read enough about suicide to know that when someone has formed a plan, there may be little loved ones can do to stop it.

As we had in his obituary, we pulled no punches about the suicide at the memorial service. And then, something rather amazing happened.

Towards the end, when thanking everyone for coming, my sister declared an intention to not feel shame that our father had killed himself.

Within seconds, all six siblings had joined her in a group hug, and when we turned around, every person in the audience was standing and clapping.

Afterwards, my aunt pulled us into a private corner while others dined in the church hall.

My father's brother, her husband, had died in 2010, also at age eighty-three, at his home in New Hampshire.

It was a death we'd been told was illness-related, but my aunt and cousin, near tears, told us our uncle had killed himself. Like my father, he shot himself in the head. He did this in their backyard, and they'd never told anyone.

Never mind the common practice of keeping it out of the obituary, they hadn't told any family members (including my father). Not co-workers, not friends. No one.

My sister's comment about shame, she said, compelled her to disclose this to us. She had felt ashamed and followed what she now saw as a misguided desire to protect my uncle's happy-go-lucky image. So she kept a secret.

"I wish I had the courage to handle it the way you did," she told us. "Because one lie led to another."

We sat in stunned silence. Two brothers, both gregarious men, had shot themselves. I try to understand their actions, but find I can't.

I do know this: If I'd returned home and pretended my

father died a natural, nontraumatic death, I would have felt not only bereft and unspeakably sad, but isolated and alone.

The truth can be a hard, unmovable object. But without it, it's impossible to get your bearings. Without the truth, there's no true comfort from others.

The surest way through grief lies in connection — in knowing you are bereaved, but not alone. The plain truth, though it may not be simple, provides a foothold.

Paul's note

On the envelope: *To the children I love so dearly, Dad Paul*

Dan, Mitch, Laurie, Mondy, Melissa,
Also Tim!

Tonight, I didn't mean to deceive you because I love you all much more than you realize. You will heal from this I know because the human mind mends fast and well. It hurts me to leave you, but I feel that I must do this so it will avoid future hurt. If I lost my mind, I'd regret that I let it happen to me, and I have to do what I feel is the correct thing for me to do. Try to understand it's a must for me to avoid future pain. With all my love I leave you. Please find happiness together. I love you. Don't let hurt destroy your happiness. You will heal and my love will help you to heal.

Your loving Dad

Paul

Lee Hawkins' letter

May 14, 2013

Dear Laurie,

I have just reread your column about your father's death, one that is headed to my folder marked DEATH. I am going to speak to you as your father might.

    For many years I have talked with my children about my determination NEVER to become a resident of a nursing home. How to handle that was not so clear, though I did and do embrace the thought of a planned death: finding a time when my loved ones are able to be with me to celebrate all that we have shared without interrupting some critical time in their own separate lives, and when they can remember me as alive, interested and as interesting as I ever was, or at least enough so to refresh their memories.

    All three of my children, I thought, had accepted the wisdom of my choice, my oldest daughter, Sue, the most appreciative of all, having now participated in her father-in-law's lingering, unplanned death. He was 94, bedridden, with no real hope for better health, yet he was not ready for any alternative living arrangement. He wanted to stay alone in his home, cook his own meals, get together with his friends, and LIVE. (Wouldn't we all?)

Still, some months ago, when I said to Sue, "I think it's about time to consider how we are going to finalize plans for my death," her reaction was "Oh, not YET." Not surprisingly, I feel the same way! There are unfinished chores: letters to write, a will to rethink. Above my husband's desk, where I am now writing, a small poster says "Life is what happens to you when you are making other plans." Life now leaves me with a desire to do those last things and very little energy to actually DO them!

I admire your father. He left you with so many warm feelings, as you did him. He was thoughtful in the papers he left behind. As a non-violent person myself I cannot imagine choosing the violence of a gunshot death and wonder that your father would leave you such an image, but he did save you the last memory of him as an old man with nothing to give, expression-less, kept alive but not living.

Suicide might be a source of shame to family members if they had in some way made life unbearable for the 'victim,' clearly not the case here.

To me, your father is a role model!

You have lost a warm, thoughtful, caring father. PEACE!

Lee (Hawkins)

Don's obituary

Published Feb 25, 2010

Donald R. Loisel, 1926-2010

DERRY, NH — Donald R. "Don"Loisel, of Derry, NH, passed away Tuesday, Feb. 16, 2010 at his home.

He was born in Waterville, Maine, and was the son of the late Pierre and Yvette (Bourque) Loisel.

Don was raised and educated in Waterville. He later relocated to New Hampshire, after proudly serving his country during World War II with the U. S. Navy. He served on the USS *Chicago* and was one of the first people to go through the Panama Canal. Don was proud and honored to be a veteran and loved his country and flag.

Don was retired and had worked for 27 years as a Facilities Supervisor for Sanders Associates in Nashua, NH. He was a member of the V. F. W. Post 1617 and American Legion Post 9, both of Derry.

Don is survived by his wife, Joanne P. (Calderone) Loisel; daughters, Suzanne D. Saindon and her husband Mark of Chicago, and Kelley Belley; one son, David Loisel; and a brother, Paul Loisel of Maine. There are also several nieces and nephews. He was also the brother of the late Carl Loisel.

ARRANGEMENTS: Family and friends may call on Thursday, Feb. 18, 2010 from 6 to 9 P.M. at the Cataudella Funeral Home, 126 Pleasant Valley St., Methuen. Funeral Mass of Christian Burial will be celebrated on Friday, Feb. 19, 2010 at 10 A.M. in Corpus Christi Parish at Holy Rosary Church, 35 Essex St., Lawrence. Burial will follow in Elmwood Cemetery, Methuen. In lieu of flowers memorial donations may be made in Don's memory to the V. F. W. Post 1617, 18 Railroad Ave., Derry, NH 03038.

Paul's obituary

Published Dec. 5, 2012

Paul Reginald Loisel, 1928 – 2012

AUGUSTA — Paul Reginald Loisel, 83, died Dec. 3 the way he lived his life — on his own terms. Paul spent a joyful evening having a belated Thanksgiving dinner with his family, during which time many stories were told and many laughs were shared. Later that night, Paul took his own life.

Paul was born Dec. 27, 1928, in Waterville, the middle son of Yvette and Philip Loisel.

He graduated from Waterville High School in 1946; the same year he joined the Navy, where he served for two years. Upon his return to Waterville, he attended Thomas College, graduating in 1950. He married Marlene Cote, and the couple had five children, Timothy, Daniel, Alan, Michaela and Laurie. They were married for about 13 years.

In 1969, Paul did something that was unusual for a father in that day and age: He successfully sought custody of his five children. At that point, he married Rosalind Mains, and adopted her daughter, Rosamond. Together, Rosalind and Paul had a daughter, Melissa.

Over the course of his working life, Paul was a hard

worker with a feisty, entrepreneurial spirit. He was a self-employed salesman, peddling bread and then milk and for 13 years; he sold Baby Butlers all around the state of Maine. The family lived for a time in East Vassalboro, where Paul decided to try his hand at chicken farming. After a year as tenant farmers, Paul and Rosalind bought a farm in Pittston in 1971. They successfully ran that farm, raising broiling hens for about 15 years. Throughout his life, Paul launched assorted business enterprises, among them a thriving roadside vegetable stand on the farm in Pittston that was staffed by his children. After the farm closed when the chicken business moved out of Maine, Paul worked various jobs, including at the Maine Turnpike Authority and for a painting company and for 20 years he worked at the former Associated Grocers of Maine. After his retirement, it was hard for Paul to sit still. He loved to dance more than anything. He sold cremation packages and educated people about the value of cremation. He drove a car with a license plate that read "Cremate." Also during his retirement, Paul was an avid reader, took a variety of classes at the University of Maine and was an enthusiastic, almost evangelical, atheist.

Throughout his life, Paul was always proud of his children. And they loved him deeply.

Paul was predeceased by his brothers, Don and Carl; his ex-wife, Marlene; and his son, Alan. He leaves his children Timothy, Daniel (Kathy), Michaela, Laurie (Lydia Rackenberg), Rosamond Stevens (John) and Melissa Curtis (Ed); his former wife and longtime friend, Rosalind Loisel; many grandchildren and great-grandchildren, who affectionately called him "Pépère;" and nieces and nephews.

A memorial service will be at 11 A.M. Saturday, Dec. 8, in the Unitarian Universalist Community Church, 69 Winthrop St.

Lee's obituary

Published September 13, 2014

Eleanor "Lee" (Hart) Hawkins, 1924 – 2014

NORTHAMPTON — Eleanor "Lee" (Hart) Hawkins, 90, an educator and community activist, died Tuesday, Sept. 2, 2014, at her Northampton home in the Lathrop Communities.

The daughter of Mabel (Bauer) and Robert Hart, she was born Feb. 13, 1924, in San Jose, California, and grew up primarily in Carmel, close to the ocean.

She was predeceased by her husband Roger, and is survived by children Sue and her husband Wayne, Jeremy and Rebecca, grandchildren Jessica and Justin Hawkins, and great-granddaughter Mya Ray.

She graduated from the University of California Berkeley and received her master's degree from Bank Street College of Education.

Lee was known for her ready smile and willingness to help those in need. Lee inherited an adventurous spirit from her parents, and honed it while traveling across the country as a teenager with family friends.

After college, she went to Maine to work as a summer camp counselor, an unintended permanent move to the east coast. She moved to New York City and worked for Travelers Aid Society where she met Roger Hawkins who would become her husband. In 1948, she went on a yearlong solo journey to post-war Europe, hosteling and traveling primarily on her 3-speed bike through England, Scotland, Italy, the Netherlands, and Sweden (where she settled in as a nanny).

Lee returned to New York City and married Roger in 1950. She worked as a comparison shopper for Macy's and did her student teaching at Downtown Community School, an experimental, cooperative and racially integrated school. There she met her educational soul mate and lifelong friend, Grace Ilchuk and the folksinger Pete Seeger who helped shape her commitment to social action.

Rog and Lee moved to Staten Island, where they raised their family. They joined the Unitarian Church of Staten Island, where Lee found kindred spirits. Lee had a fulfilling career as a public school teacher for 18 years, instigated community projects that benefited kids of all ages, organized Camp Fire Girls groups, and served as the director of religious education, chairman of the social concerns committee and president of her church. She brought to her family rich educational experiences and happy memories of camping, creating impressive parade floats and costumes, dramatic-thematic birthday parties, folk dancing, singing, and 'making do' on a shoestring.

In 1991, Lee and Roger moved to Northampton, settling in the Lathrop Community, and diving headlong into the activities and community of the Unitarian Society of Northampton and Florence. Among many other things, Lee made food for the homeless shelter, worked on the Living Wage Campaign and was a devoted member of the Social Justice Committee. She worked with prison inmates in Springfield, using a decisional training program and was an avid supporter of the Treehouse Community for foster families in Easthampton. She was never shy about sharing her opinions, but listened readily to others.

Lee advocated for quality of life, and Death with Dignity. In August, she did what she had long planned: Feeling that she had lived a good, long life and was ready to move on, she stopped eating and drinking. Over the following two weeks, with caring support from Cooley Dickinson Hospice 'angels,' she spent many loving hours with her children, grandchildren, and friends from her beloved community. She died Tuesday, Sept. 2, with her children holding her hands, drifting off as a hospice harpist played.

The celebration of lee's Life will be held Saturday, Sept. 27, at 3 P.M. at the Unitarian Society of Northampton, with reception to follow.

Memorial contributions may be made to Hospice of Cooley Dickinson, 168 Industrial Drive, Northampton, MA 01060, or to Treehouse Foundation, attn: Judy Cockerton, 1 Treehouse Circle, Easthampton, MA 01027.

Discussion prompts

Lee Hawkins felt it was essential that people think about how they might want their final days to unfold. The following questions may prompt discussions on the issues raised.

1. Lee and Paul expressed similar feelings about wanting a sense of agency at the end of their lives, yet they found vastly different ways to gain control. What is your reaction to how each of them approached this need?

2. The method Lee used to bring about her death, voluntarily stopping eating and drinking, known as VSED, is legal across the country. Other steps that require assistance to bring about death are not legal except in states that have passed laws with specific criteria outlined in the legislation. Variously called compassionate medical aid in dying, assisted suicide, Death with Dignity, and assisted death, these laws are hotly contested and provoke emotional debates. What are your feelings about such deaths?

3. Death with Dignity laws apply only to people with specific terminal diagnoses, not to people like Lee and Paul facing the slow and natural decline of old age with no diagnosis other than human mortality. Do they have a right to hasten their deaths when living has become something they no longer want?

4. In the final chapter, Laurie wonders if the family's efforts to find "fixes" to the circumstances in Paul's life that ultimately led to his suicide, created distance between Paul and his children. What are your thoughts about that?

5. One of Lee's friends wondered if Lee wouldn't have made the choice she made if the community had provided more support sooner. What are your thoughts about that?

6. Just as Lee was about to enact her plan to stop eating and drinking, she was asked to see a psychiatrist. What do you think about that request from the hospice organization caring for her?

7. Lee postponed the date on which she planned to stop eating and drinking a few times. What is your reaction to this?

8. How do you feel about the newspaper publishing a picture of Lee after she died?

9. If you have been involved in decision-making with someone nearing the end of life, did you feel the medical provider helped by facilitating conversations about treatment options — including the choice to have no treatment at all?

10. In the chapter "After Lee," Lee's friends talk about the feelings her actions brought up in them and how those feelings changed. One friend who felt angry at the time said her feelings evolved a year later. Another friend said Lee's fearlessness helped her sort through her own thinking about how she might approach her final years. Have you thought about your final years, or those of a loved one?

11. Do the choices Lee and Paul made prompt you to reconsider anything?

12. Will you initiate conversations with loved ones about your or their death? If not, what stops you? If so, how do you imagine it will go?

Acknowledgments

For being such a solitary, and, yes, sometimes lonely activity, writing can be an amazing testament to community. That was my experience working in a daily newsroom for twenty-nine years, where I learned the role collaboration and teamwork play in the creative process. That's also been my experience and great good fortune in writing this book.

    Which leads me to my many heartfelt thank-yous. Words simply fail me here, but they're all I have.

    Thank you to the Hawkins clan, Lee, Jerry, Sue and Becky, for trusting me with your family's inspiring story. Thank you to the Loisels, Paul, Tim, Dan, Alan, Michaela, Mondy and Melissa, for letting me be your scribe all these years — also for understanding that even though what's on these pages may not be your exact truth, there is a truth here.

    Thanks to Lydia Rackenberg for your enthusiasm when I was writing the stories about Lee, for joining me in welcoming her into our family, and for your belief in this book.

    Thanks go to Jean Ryan and Dr. Jeff Zesiger, who supported this project when they were at VNA & Hospice of Cooley Dickinson Health Care and I was at the Daily Hampshire Gazette, and to the Gazette for permission to reprint (with some modifications) chapters 6, 7 and 9 which were published in the paper Sept. 23, 24, 25, 2014.

As for the creation of this book: Thanks to Christine Sass and Steve Simmer for suggesting Lee's story should be made into a book so folks might discuss the issues it raised, and to Lore Detenber who absolutely insisted the combination of my father's death and how it led to my relationship with Lee would be a book people would want to read.

Thank you to the congregation of the Unitarian Society of Northampton and Florence who let me report about Lee without ever trying to tell me how to do it or what to say (or not say) and to the Rev. Janet Bush for the very same.

As for the writing of this book: Thank you to all the women, past and present, in my long-running writing group, where for years I worked over this material without quite realizing that's what I was doing. Your laughter, camaraderie and joy in writing has been a gift.

Thank you to author and friend M B Caschetta for reading a very early version and making incisive comments about the writing, structure and title in the kindest possible way that put me on the exact right path. To Dora Lewis, Phoebe Mitchell, Michaela Loisel, Dan Loisel and Sydney Rackenberg-Loisel for reading early versions and helping me with encouragement, questions and excellent suggestions. Thanks to Chris Young, Barbara Solow, Lynn Ferro, Andria

Wolf and Simon Rackzelle for encouragment and support.

My gratitude to my dear friend and beloved colleague Suzanne Wilson knows no bounds. I invited her into the weeds with me and she happily joined me there, providing insightful suggestions about structure that led me to rearrange the order of chapters entirely and about finer points of wording that were unfailingly on-target. She asked questions and more questions, drawing out more details and more story. Our professional relationship meant the world to me at the paper; that we could continue it years later was a surprise and delight. Our work together reminds me that everything, from food to political action, to the lonely act of writing, is better in community.

My thanks also to Carol Lollis, an incredible photographer, journalist and friend. There's nothing like a great collaboration between a reporter and photographer. When it turns into a friendship, well, it's the bomb.

Thanks to Carin Clevidence, Jeff Zesiger, Jonathan Harr, Janet Bush, M B Caschetta and Rev. Karen Johnston who generously agreed to read a draft and write their thoughts down for me to invite people to read this book, which I was honored to do.

To Steve Strimer for his gentle encouragement of this project, to Anna Mullen for her sensitive editorial eye and elegant sense of design, and to Levellers Press for taking this book on, thank you!

A few more individual appreciations are necessary: to Sue and Becky Hawkins for your friendship and support, to the sisterhood of Lee Hawkins' Traveling Pants, Janet Spongberg, Patricia Wright, Heather Johnson, and to Sue and Becky. And most of all my love and thanks to Lydia, Simon and Sydney, who every day, wherever you are, help me feel the meaning of the words 'I'm home.'

November 2019

LAURIE LOISEL is a freelance journalist in Northampton, Massachusetts.